RICE A RONI & NOODLE RONI

THE SAN FRANCISCO TREAT

Recipes for Busy Cooks

PUBLICATIONS INTERNATIONAL, LTD.

RICE-A-RONI® and NOODLE RONI® are registered trademarks of The
Golden Grain Company, a subsidiary of The Quaker Oats Company.

AUNT JEMIMA® and QUAKER CORNMEAL® are registered trademarks
of The Quaker Oats Company.

This edition published by Publications International, Ltd.,
7373 N. Cicero Ave., Lincolnwood, IL 60646.

Photography: Sacco Productions Limited, Chicago

Pictured on the front cover: Paella a la Española (*page 30*).

Pictured on the back cover (*top to bottom*): Country Chicken Dinner
(*page 18*), Glazed Pork & Rice (*page 42*) and Cheesy Chicken & Rice
Florentine (*page 44*).

ISBN: 0-7853-1196-3

Manufactured in U.S.A.

8 7 6 5 4 3 2 1

Nutritional Analysis: Nutritional information is given for the recipes in
this publication. Each analysis is based on the food items in the ingredient
list, except ingredients labeled as "optional" or "for garnish." When more
than one ingredient choice is listed, the first ingredient was used for
analysis. If a range for the amount of an ingredient was given, the
nutritional analysis was based on the lowest amount. If a range is given
in the yield of a recipe, the higher yield was used to calculate the per
serving information. Foods offered as "serve with" suggestions are not
included in the analysis unless otherwise stated.

Microwave Cooking: Microwave ovens vary in wattage. The microwave
cooking times in this publication are approximate. Use the cooking times
as guidelines and check for doneness before adding more time.

RICE A RONI & NOODLE RONI

THE SAN FRANCISCO TREAT

Recipes for Busy Cooks

INTRODUCTION & HELPFUL HINTS

RECIPES FOR BUSY COOKS!

It seems like our schedules are getting busier and busier every day. With so much going on, it's becoming harder to plan and prepare tasty, healthy meals your family enjoys, and are convenient enough for your hectic schedule. That's why the makers of Rice-A-Roni® and Noodle Roni® developed **Recipes for Busy Cooks!** Both products are already convenient to prepare as a side dish, but with these easy recipes you can prepare wholesome and delicious main dishes as well.

Recipes for Busy Cooks! features over 50 quick and easy recipes for delicious main meals your family will love. Most are ready in 30 minutes or less and use quick preparation methods like stir-fry, or only need one pan for easy clean up! Each recipe has easy-to-follow step-by-step instructions. And for those occasions when you're really pressed for time, we've also included a chart of easy Stir-In ideas on page 10; it's a great way to use leftovers!

Every delicious recipe combines the great taste of Rice-A-Roni® or Noodle Roni® with a short list of ingredients you probably already have in your pantry. With a wide variety of international flavors from Paella a la Española to Lemon-Garlic Chicken & Rice, you can create exciting new dinner favorites for your family. Or, for a twist on an American classic, try our Southwestern Chicken. **Recipes for Busy Cooks!** provides recipes for many of your family's favorite Rice-A-Roni® and Noodle Roni® flavors, so every recipe is sure to please!

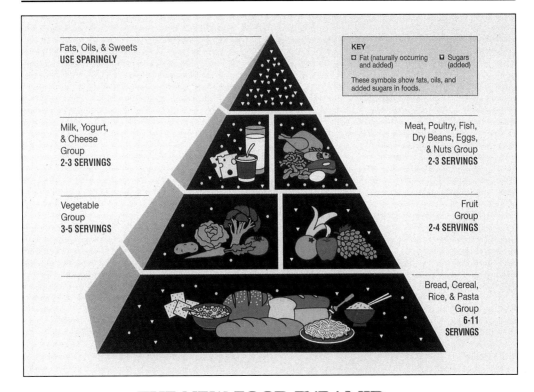

THE NEW FOOD PYRAMID
Changing How we think About Food

All of us who grew up on the 4 Basic Food Groups learned to plan our meals around meat. New research has shown that foods rich in complex carbohydrates are more important than we thought, and that meat protein, while good, can carry more fat and cholesterol than we need. To help plan healthier meals the USDA created The Food Pyramid: A Guide to Daily Food Choices.

Focus on Carbohydrates

The base of the new pyramid is rice, pasta, cereal and bread. These complex carbohydrates are low in fat and cholesterol, rich in vitamins and minerals, and taste great too! Plan meals around two or more servings of these, plus vegetables and/or fruit, then balance with other essentials such as lean meat, poultry and low fat dairy items. Use sweets, salts and fat sparingly. Remember this is just a guide to help plan healthier meals. The number of portions and servings will vary depending on size, age and sex of the eater.

What's a Serving?

Here are a few examples of the USDA's serving recommendations:
Rice, Pasta, Bread, Cereal: ½ cup cooked cereal, pasta, rice, noodles, 1 slice bread, ½ bagel
Vegetables: 1 cup leafy greens, ½ cup raw or cooked vegetables
Fruit: 1 apple, 1 banana, ¾ cup of juice, ½ cup cut-up fruit
Dairy: 1 cup low fat milk, 1 cup yogurt, ½ ounce hard cheese, ½ cup cottage cheese
Meat, Dry Beans: 1 to 3 ounces cooked lean meat, poultry or fish, 1 cup cooked beans, 2 eggs, 4 teaspoons peanut butter

PANTRY-STOCKING TIP SHEET

A well-stocked pantry can make the difference when it comes to preparing an easy and nutritious meal. To help today's busy cooks avoid the "what can I make for dinner tonight" blues, the kitchen experts from Rice-A-Roni® and Noodle Roni® brands have developed the following list of basic cooking items to help ensure some degree of preparedness for last minute cooks. A few items from each category can be selected according to buyer preference to ensure that there will always be something to eat for dinner. When combined with Rice-A-Roni® or Noodle Roni® products, these ingredients can be turned into a satisfying, quick and easy main dish meal in no time at all.

FRUITS
apples
lemons
oranges
raisins

VEGETABLES
canned corn
canned green beans
canned tomatoes
canned tomato sauce
celery
cucumber
fresh broccoli
fresh carrots
fresh mushrooms
fresh potatoes
fresh tomatoes
frozen broccoli
frozen corn
frozen mixed vegetables
frozen peas
garlic
green or red bell peppers
lettuce
onions

DAIRY
2% milk
American cheese
cheddar cheese
cream cheese
margarine
parmesan cheese

MEATS/POULTRY/FISH
bacon
beef steaks
canned tuna
chicken breasts or turkey
  breast
chicken pieces (other than
  breasts)
eggs
frankfurters
ground beef or ground
  turkey
pork chops

**CANNED OR PACKAGED
  FOODS**
barbecue sauce
canned beans (red kidney
  etc.)
catsup
cider vinegar
cornstarch
Dijon mustard
mayonnaise
no-stick cooking spray
nuts (no pistachio, cashews
  or macadamia)
olive oil
pourable salad dressing
regular soy sauce
spaghetti sauce
stewed tomatoes
stir-fry sauce

tomato paste
tomato sauce
white distilled vinegar
Worcestershire sauce
yellow mustard

FROZEN FOODS
frozen broccoli
frozen corn
frozen fish (not breaded)
frozen green beans
frozen mixed vegetables
frozen orange juice
frozen peas
frozen spinach

**SPICES/HERBS/
  EXTRACTS/
  FLAVORINGS**
basil
bay leaf
black pepper
dill weed
garlic powder
ground ginger
ground sage
instant minced onion
Italian seasonings
oregano
paprika
parsley flakes
red pepper (crushed or
  ground)
thyme

COOKING TIPS

CHICKEN PREPARATION TIPS

• To easily cook chicken for use in recipes that call for chopped cooked chicken, microwave 1 pound boneless skinless chicken breasts, covered, on HIGH 7 to 8 minutes. If chicken is still pink, continue to microwave at 1 minute intervals until it is no longer pink in center.

• About 1¼ pounds of chicken breast meat *or* a 3-pound broiler-fryer yields about 2 cups chopped cooked chicken.

DONENESS TESTS FOR CHICKEN

Following are several ways to determine if chicken is thoroughly cooked and ready to eat:

• To test bone-in chicken pieces, insert a fork into chicken. It should go in with ease and juices should run clear. Meat and juices nearest bones may still be a little pink even though chicken is cooked thoroughly.

• Boneless chicken pieces are done when centers are no longer pink; test this by cutting into chicken with a knife.

SEAFOOD PREPARATION TIPS

• Frozen shrimp and scallops should be thawed in the refrigerator before cooking.

PEELING AND DEVEINING SHRIMP

Shrimp may be peeled and deveined either before or after cooking.

• To peel shrimp, shell is easily removed with your fingers. Start peeling shell on legs side. Lift shell up and over, then back around to other leg side. Remove tail section or leave it on, depending on how shrimp are being used.

• To devein shrimp, make a small cut along back; lift out dark vein with tip of a knife under cold running water. Special gadgets make peeling and deveining shrimp a one-step process.

DONENESS TESTS FOR SEAFOOD

• Fish: Fish is done when it flakes easily when tested with a fork at thickest part, fish turns opaque or milky white and internal temperature of fish is 145°F.

• Shrimp: In or out of shell, shrimp is done when it turns pink and is firm.

• Scallops: Scallops are done when they turn opaque or milky white and are firm.

EASY STIR-IN CHART
To prepare a fast and easy Rice-A-Roni® dinner for four, *choose ONE selection from each of the 4 groups and follow these simple directions:*

1. Prepare Rice-A-Roni® Mix as package directs, stirring in your selected meat, vegetable and

RICE-A-RONI®	+POULTRY, MEAT, FISH	
	2 cups chopped cooked chicken *or* turkey	
Broccoli Au Gratin, Broccoli Au Gratin With ⅓ Less Salt	2 cups thinly sliced cooked steak *or* 2½ cups chopped cooked pork	
	2 cans (6⅛ ounces *each*) tuna, drained, flaked	
Chicken **Chicken With ⅓ Less Salt** **Chicken & Vegetables** **Chicken & Mushrooms** **Chicken & Broccoli**	2 cups chopped cooked chicken *or* turkey	
	2 cans (6⅛ ounces *each*) tuna, drained, flaked	
Beef **Beef & Mushrooms**	2 cups cooked and drained ground beef *or* 2 cups thinly sliced cooked steak *or* 2½ cups chopped cooked pork	
Herb & Butter **Pilaf** **Fried Rice** **Fried Rice With ⅓ Less Salt** **Long Grain & Wild Original** **Spanish**	2 cups chopped cooked chicken *or* turkey	
	2 cups cooked and drained ground beef *or* 2 cups thinly sliced cooked steak *or* 2½ cups chopped cooked pork	
	2 cans (6⅛ ounces *each*) tuna, drained, flaked	

seasoning during last 10 minutes of cooking.
2. Continue cooking as package directs or until vegetables are tender and heated through.
3. Sprinkle with parmesan or cheddar cheese before serving, if desired

+VEGETABLE 	+SEASONING 
2 cups broccoli flowerets *or* **1 package (10 ounces)** frozen chopped broccoli *or* **2 cups** sliced mushrooms *or* **2 cups** frozen mixed vegetables	⅛ **teaspoon** garlic powder *or* ⅛ **teaspoon** crushed red pepper flakes *or* **1 teaspoon** lemon juice
1 package (10 ounces) frozen chopped broccoli *or* **1 package (10 ounces)** frozen peas and carrots *or* **2 cups** sliced mushrooms	⅛ **teaspoon** garlic powder *or* **1 teaspoon** dried basil *or* **1 teaspoon** oregano leaves
1 cup chopped onion *and* **1 cup** chopped green bell pepper *or* **1 cup** frozen peas *or* **1 cup** sliced celery	⅛ **teaspoon** garlic powder *or* ⅛ **teaspoon** dill weed *or* **1 teaspoon** lemon juice
1 cup chopped onion *and* **1 cup** broccoli flowerets *or* **1 cup** frozen chopped broccoli *or* **1 cup** chopped green pepper	⅛ **teaspoon** crushed red pepper flakes *or* **1 teaspoon** dried oregano leaves *or* **1 teaspoon** soy sauce
1 cup chopped onion *and* **1 cup** chopped green bell pepper *or* **1 cup** frozen peas *or* **1 cup** sliced celery	⅛ **teaspoon** dill weed *or* ⅛ **teaspoon** garlic powder *or* **1 teaspoon** lemon juice
2 cups *or* **1 package (10 ounces)** frozen green beans *or* **2 cups** frozen mixed vegetables *or* **1 cup** chopped green bell pepper *and* **1 cup** chopped onion	⅛ **teaspoon** garlic powder *or* **1 teaspoon** dried oregano leaves *or* **1 teaspoon** Worcestershire *or* **1 teaspoon** soy sauce
1 cup chopped onion *and* **1 cup** broccoli flowerets *or* **1 cup** frozen chopped broccoli *or* **1 cup** frozen peas and carrots *or* **1 cup** chopped green bell pepper	⅛ **teaspoon** crushed red pepper flakes *or* **1 teaspoon** dried oregano leaves *or* **1 teaspoon** soy sauce
2 cups *or* **1 package (10 ounces)** frozen green beans *or* **2 cups** frozen mixed vegetables *or* **1 cup** chopped green bell pepper *and* **1 cup** chopped onion	⅛ **teaspoon** garlic powder *or* **1 teaspoon** dried oregano leaves *or* **1 teaspoon** Worcestershire *or* **1 teaspoon** soy sauce
1 cup chopped onion *and* **1 cup** chopped green bell pepper *or* **1 cup** frozen peas *or* **1 cup** sliced celery	⅛ **teaspoon** dill weed *or* ⅛ **teaspoon** garlic powder *or* **1 teaspoon** lemon juice

ONE-PAN MEALS

LEMON-GARLIC CHICKEN & RICE

Serve with a tossed green salad.

4 skinless, boneless chicken breast halves
1 teaspoon paprika
Salt and pepper (optional)
2 tablespoons margarine or butter
2 cloves garlic, minced
1 package (6.9 ounces) RICE-A-RONI Chicken Flavor
2 tablespoons lemon juice
1 cup chopped red or green bell pepper
½ teaspoon grated lemon peel

1. Sprinkle chicken with paprika, salt and pepper.

2. In large skillet, melt margarine over medium-high heat. Add chicken and garlic; cook 2 minutes on each side or until browned. Remove from skillet; set aside, reserving drippings. Keep warm.

3. In same skillet, sauté rice-vermicelli mix in reserved drippings over medium heat, until vermicelli is golden brown. Stir in 2¼ cups water, lemon juice and contents of seasoning packet. Top rice with chicken; bring to a boil over high heat.

4. Cover; reduce heat. Simmer 10 minutes. Stir in red pepper and lemon peel.

5. Cover; continue to simmer 10 minutes or until liquid is absorbed, rice is tender and chicken is no longer pink inside.   *4 servings*

Nutrition Information: ¼ RECIPE

Calories	360	Sodium	850 mg
Total Fat	8 g	Total Carbohydrates	39 g
Saturated Fat	1 g	Dietary Fiber	2 g
Cholesterol	70 mg	Protein	33 g

% Daily Value:

Vitamin A	41%	Calcium	4%
Vitamin C	87%	Iron	22%

Lemon-Garlic Chicken & Rice

JAZZY JAMBALAYA

A traditional Bayou recipe in half the time.

1 package (6.8 ounces) RICE-A-RONI Spanish Rice
1 cup chopped cooked chicken *or* ham
1 cup chopped onion
1 cup chopped green bell pepper
2 cloves garlic, minced
3 tablespoons vegetable oil
1 can (14½ ounces) tomatoes, undrained, chopped
Dash hot pepper sauce (optional)
½ pound raw shrimp, shelled, deveined *or* 8 ounces frozen cleaned precooked shrimp

1. In large skillet, combine rice-vermicelli mix, chicken, onion, green pepper, garlic and oil. Sauté over medium heat, stirring frequently until vermicelli is golden brown.

2. Stir in 2 cups water, tomatoes, hot pepper sauce and contents of seasoning packet; bring to a boil over high heat.

3. Cover; reduce heat. Simmer 10 minutes.

4. Stir in shrimp.

5. Cover; continue cooking 8 to 10 minutes or until liquid is absorbed, rice is tender and shrimp turn pink.
5 servings

Nutrition Information: ⅕ RECIPE

Calories	330	Sodium	600 mg
Total Fat	12 g	Total Carbohydrates	37 g
Saturated Fat	2 g	Dietary Fiber	3 g
Cholesterol	80 mg	Protein	21 g

% Daily Value:

Vitamin A	15%	Calcium	8%
Vitamin C	57%	Iron	26%

CHICKEN DIVAN

Only six ingredients make up this one-dish meal.

⅔ cup milk
2 tablespoons margarine or butter
1 package (4.8 ounces) NOODLE RONI Corkscrew Pasta with Four Cheeses
2 cups chopped cooked chicken or turkey
2 cups broccoli flowerets
½ cup croutons, coarsely crushed

1. In round 3-quart microwaveable glass casserole, combine 1½ cups water, milk and margarine. Microwave, uncovered, on HIGH 4 to 5 minutes or until boiling.

2. Stir in pasta, contents of seasoning packet, chicken and broccoli.

3. Microwave, uncovered, on HIGH 12 to 13 minutes, stirring after 6 minutes.

4. Let stand 4 to 5 minutes or until desired consistency. Sauce will be thin, but will thicken upon standing. Stir before serving.

5. Sprinkle with croutons.
4 servings

Nutrition Information: ¼ RECIPE

Calories	370	Sodium	525 mg
Total Fat	15 g	Total Carbohydrates	30 g
Saturated Fat	4 g	Dietary Fiber	4 g
Cholesterol	70 mg	Protein	29 g

% Daily Value:

Vitamin A	27%	Calcium	16%
Vitamin C	78%	Iron	19%

Jazzy Jambalaya

HUNGARIAN GOULASH STEW

Serve this one-dish stew with pumpernickel bread.

³⁄₄ pound lean ground beef (80% lean)
¹⁄₂ cup chopped onion
1 clove garlic, minced
1 package (4.8 ounces) NOODLE RONI Angel Hair Pasta with Herbs
1 can (14¹⁄₂ ounces) diced tomatoes, undrained
1 cup frozen corn *or* 1 can (8 ounces) whole kernel corn, drained
1¹⁄₂ teaspoons paprika
¹⁄₈ teaspoon black pepper
Sour cream (optional)

1. In 3-quart saucepan, brown ground beef, onion and garlic; drain.

2. Add 1¹⁄₃ cups water, pasta, contents of seasoning packet, tomatoes, frozen corn and seasonings. Bring just to a boil.

3. Reduce heat to medium.

4. Boil, uncovered, stirring frequently, 5 to 6 minutes or until pasta is tender.

5. Let stand 3 minutes or until desired consistency. Stir before serving. Serve with sour cream, if desired. *4 servings*

Nutrition Information: ¹⁄₄ RECIPE

Calories	360	Sodium	625 mg
Total Fat	14 g	Total Carbohydrates	39 g
Saturated Fat	5 g	Dietary Fiber	3 g
Cholesterol	50 mg	Protein	22 g
% Daily Value:			
Vitamin A	24%	Calcium	6%
Vitamin C	34%	Iron	27%

HOT TACO SALAD

Salsa adds lots of flavor to this warm salad.

³⁄₄ pound lean ground beef (80% lean)
¹⁄₂ cup chopped onion
1 package (6.8 ounces) RICE-A-RONI Beef Flavor
¹⁄₂ cup salsa
1 teaspoon chili powder
4 cups shredded lettuce
1 medium tomato, chopped
¹⁄₂ cup (2 ounces) shredded monterey jack or cheddar cheese
¹⁄₂ cup crushed tortilla chips (optional)

1. In large skillet, brown ground beef and onion; drain. Remove from skillet; set aside.

2. In same skillet, prepare Rice-A-Roni Mix as package directs.

3. Stir in meat mixture, salsa and chili powder; continue cooking over low heat 3 to 4 minutes or until heated through.

4. Arrange lettuce on serving platter. Top with rice mixture, tomato and cheese. Top with tortilla chips, if desired.

5 servings

Nutrition Information: ¹⁄₅ RECIPE

Calories	380	Sodium	900 mg
Total Fat	18 g	Total Carbohydrates	34 g
Saturated Fat	4 g	Dietary Fiber	2 g
Cholesterol	51 mg	Protein	20 g
% Daily Value:			
Vitamin A	36%	Calcium	14%
Vitamin C	52%	Iron	26%

Hot Taco Salad

COUNTRY CHICKEN DINNER

Prepare this satisfying meal in just 30 minutes.

¼ **cup milk**
2 **tablespoons margarine or butter**
1 **package (4.7 ounces) NOODLE RONI Linguine Pasta with Chicken & Broccoli**
2 **cups frozen mixed broccoli, cauliflower and carrots vegetable medley**
2 **cups chopped cooked chicken or turkey**
1 **teaspoon dried basil**

1. In round 3-quart microwaveable glass casserole, combine 1¾ cups water, milk and margarine. Microwave, uncovered, on HIGH 4 to 5 minutes or until boiling.

2. Gradually add pasta while stirring.

3. Stir in contents of seasoning packet, frozen vegetables, chicken and basil.

4. Microwave, uncovered, on HIGH 14 to 15 minutes, stirring gently after 7 minutes. Sauce will be thin, but will thicken upon standing.

5. Let stand 4 to 5 minutes or until desired consistency. Stir before serving.   *4 servings*

Nutrition Information: ¼ RECIPE

Calories	340	Sodium	525 mg
Total Fat	13 g	Total Carbohydrates	28 g
Saturated Fat	3 g	Dietary Fiber	3 g
Cholesterol	65 mg	Protein	27 g

% Daily Value:

Vitamin A	112%	Calcium	8%
Vitamin C	53%	Iron	21%

BACON-TUNA PARMESANO

Serve a tossed green salad with this easy dinner.

½ **cup milk**
2 **tablespoons margarine or butter**
1 **package (4.8 ounces) NOODLE RONI Parmesano**
1 **package (10 ounces) frozen peas**
1 **can (6⅛ ounces) white tuna in water, drained, flaked**
4 **slices crisply cooked bacon, crumbled**
½ **cup sliced green onions**

1. In round 3-quart microwaveable glass casserole, combine 1⅔ cups water, milk and margarine. Microwave, uncovered, on HIGH 4 to 5 minutes or until boiling.

2. Stir in pasta, contents of seasoning packet, frozen peas, tuna, bacon and onions.

3. Microwave, uncovered, on HIGH 9 to 10 minutes or until peas are tender, stirring after 3 minutes.

4. Cover; let stand 3 to 4 minutes. Sauce will thicken upon standing. Stir before serving.   *4 servings*

Nutrition Information: ¼ RECIPE

Calories	340	Sodium	775 mg
Total Fat	12 g	Total Carbohydrates	34 g
Saturated Fat	3 g	Dietary Fiber	4 g
Cholesterol	30 mg	Protein	24 g

% Daily Value:

Vitamin A	17%	Calcium	10%
Vitamin C	30%	Iron	31%

Country Chicken Dinner

ANGEL HAIR CARBONARA

Serve this Italian specialty with crusty rolls.

²⁄₃ cup milk
2 tablespoons margarine or
   butter
1 package (4.8 ounces)
   NOODLE RONI Angel Hair
   Pasta with Herbs
2 cups chopped cooked pork or
   ham
1 package (10 ounces) frozen
   peas
¼ cup sliced green onions

1. In round 3-quart microwaveable glass casserole, combine 1½ cups water, milk and margarine. Microwave, uncovered, on HIGH 4 to 5 minutes or until boiling.

2. Gradually add pasta while stirring. Separate pasta with a fork, if needed.

3. Stir in contents of seasoning packet.

4. Microwave, uncovered, on HIGH 4 minutes, stirring gently after 2 minutes. Separate pasta with a fork, if needed. Stir in pork, frozen peas and onions. Continue to microwave 2 to 3 minutes. Sauce will be very thin, but will thicken upon standing.

5. Let stand 3 minutes or until desired consistency. Stir before serving. *4 servings*

Nutrition Information: ¼ RECIPE

Calories	430	Sodium	625 mg
Total Fat	19 g	Total Carbohydrates	36 g
Saturated Fat	6 g	Dietary Fiber	4 g
Cholesterol	65 mg	Protein	29 g

% Daily Value:

Vitamin A	17%	Calcium	10%
Vitamin C	25%	Iron	23%

CHICKEN PAPRIKASH

A quick classic Hungarian dish.

2 tablespoons margarine or
   butter
1 pound skinless, boneless
   chicken breasts or thighs,
   cut into 1-inch pieces
½ cup chopped onion
1 clove garlic, minced
1 tablespoon paprika
½ cup milk
1 package (4.7 ounces)
   NOODLE RONI Fettuccine
1 medium green bell pepper,
   cut into strips
½ cup sour half and half or sour
   cream

1. In large skillet, melt margarine over medium heat. Add chicken, onion and garlic; cook 1 minute, stirring occasionally. Add paprika; continue cooking 2 minutes.

2. Add 1½ cups water, milk, pasta, contents of seasoning packet and green pepper. Bring just to a boil. Reduce heat to medium-low.

3. Boil, uncovered, stirring frequently, 9 to 11 minutes or until pasta is desired tenderness and chicken is no longer pink inside. Sauce will thicken upon standing. Stir in sour half and half before serving. *4 servings*

Nutrition Information: ¼ RECIPE

Calories	380	Sodium	575 mg
Total Fat	15 g	Total Carbohydrates	27 g
Saturated Fat	5 g	Dietary Fiber	2 g
Cholesterol	80 mg	Protein	34 g

% Daily Value:

Vitamin A	32%	Calcium	12%
Vitamin C	35%	Iron	20%

Angel Hair Carbonara

CANTONESE BEEF & BROCCOLI

Faster than a trip for Chinese take-out!

¾ **pound cooked steak or deli roast beef, cut into thin strips**
1½ **tablespoons reduced-sodium or regular soy sauce**
1 **package (6.8 ounces) RICE-A-RONI Beef Flavor**
2 **tablespoons margarine or butter**
½ **cup chopped onion**
2 **cups broccoli flowerets**
½ **teaspoon ground ginger**

1. Toss meat with soy sauce; set aside.

2. In round 3-quart microwaveable glass casserole, combine rice-vermicelli mix, margarine and onion. Microwave, uncovered, on HIGH 4 to 5 minutes or until vermicelli is golden brown, stirring after 2 minutes.

3. Stir in 2¾ cups water and contents of seasoning packet. Cover; microwave on HIGH 11 minutes.

4. Stir in meat mixture, broccoli and ginger. Cover; microwave on HIGH 8 to 10 minutes or until most of liquid is absorbed and rice is tender.

5. Let stand 3 minutes. Stir before serving. *4 servings*

Nutrition Information: ¼ RECIPE

Calories	470	Sodium	1100 mg
Total Fat	20 g	Total Carbohydrates	41 g
Saturated Fat	6 g	Dietary Fiber	4 g
Cholesterol	75 mg	Protein	31 g

% Daily Value:

Vitamin A	29%	Calcium	6%
Vitamin C	81%	Iron	40%

SHRIMP CLASSICO

Inspired by Italian cuisine.

⅔ **cup milk**
2 **tablespoons margarine or butter**
1 **package (4.8 ounces) NOODLE RONI Angel Hair Pasta with Herbs**
1 **clove garlic, minced**
1 **package (10 ounces) frozen chopped spinach, thawed, well drained**
1 **package (10 ounces) frozen precooked shrimp, thawed, well drained**
1 **jar (2 ounces) chopped pimento, drained**

1. In 3-quart round microwaveable glass casserole, combine 1⅔ cups water, milk and margarine. Microwave, uncovered, on HIGH 4 to 5 minutes or until boiling.

2. Gradually add pasta while stirring. Separate pasta with a fork, if needed. Stir in contents of seasoning packet and garlic.

3. Microwave, uncovered, on HIGH 4 minutes, stirring gently after 2 minutes. Separate pasta with a fork, if needed. Stir in spinach, shrimp and pimento. Microwave on HIGH 1 to 2 minutes. Sauce will be very thin, but will thicken upon standing.

4. Let stand, uncovered, 2 minutes or until desired consistency. Stir before serving. *4 servings*

Nutrition Information: ¼ RECIPE

Calories	290	Sodium	725 mg
Total Fat	10 g	Total Carbohydrates	29 g
Saturated Fat	2 g	Dietary Fiber	3 g
Cholesterol	140 mg	Protein	23 g

% Daily Value:

Vitamin A	123%	Calcium	17%
Vitamin C	50%	Iron	40%

FIESTA PORK CHOPS

Cole slaw complements this dish.

4 well-trimmed ¾-inch-thick pork chops
2 teaspoons chili powder
1 tablespoon vegetable oil
1 package (6.8 ounces) RICE-A-RONI Spanish Rice
2 tablespoons margarine or butter
1 can (14½ ounces) tomatoes, undrained, chopped
½ cup chopped green bell pepper *or* 1 can (4 ounces) chopped green chiles, drained
½ cup chopped onion

1. Evenly sprinkle both sides of pork chops with chili powder. In large skillet, brown pork chops in oil over medium-high heat. Drain; set aside.

2. In same skillet, combine rice-vermicelli mix and margarine. Sauté over medium heat, stirring frequently until vermicelli is golden brown.

3. Stir in 1¾ cups water, contents of seasoning packet, tomatoes, green pepper and onion; bring to a boil over high heat.

4. Place pork chops over rice mixture; return to a boil. Cover; reduce heat. Simmer 25 to 30 minutes or until liquid is absorbed and rice and chops are tender.

4 servings

Nutrition Information: ¼ RECIPE

Calories	410	Sodium	800 mg
Total Fat	14 g	Total Carbohydrates	43 g
Saturated Fat	3 g	Dietary Fiber	4 g
Cholesterol	60 mg	Protein	28 g

% Daily Value:

Vitamin A	30%	Calcium	8%
Vitamin C	53%	Iron	27%

CHICKEN GUMBO

Serve this with corn bread.

2 tablespoons vegetable oil
¾ pound skinless, boneless chicken breasts or thighs, cut into ½-inch pieces
½ cup chopped onion
⅓ cup sliced celery
2 cloves garlic, minced
1 can (14½ ounces) tomatoes, undrained, coarsely chopped
1 can (13¾ ounces) reduced-sodium or regular chicken broth
½ cup chopped green bell pepper
½ teaspoon dried thyme leaves
⅛ teaspoon hot pepper sauce (optional)
1 bay leaf (optional)
1 package (6.8 ounces) RICE-A-RONI Spanish Rice

1. In 3-quart saucepan, heat oil over medium heat. Add chicken, onion, celery and garlic; cook 3 to 4 minutes or until chicken is no longer pink.

2. Add ¾ cup water, tomatoes, chicken broth, green pepper, thyme, hot pepper sauce, bay leaf, rice-vermicelli mix and contents of seasoning packet. Bring to a boil over high heat; reduce heat. Simmer 15 to 20 minutes or until rice is tender, stirring occasionally.

4 servings

Nutrition Information: ¼ RECIPE

Calories	370	Sodium	975 mg
Total Fat	10 g	Total Carbohydrates	44 g
Saturated Fat	2 g	Dietary Fiber	3 g
Cholesterol	50 mg	Protein	26 g

% Daily Value:

Vitamin A	17%	Calcium	8%
Vitamin C	54%	Iron	26%

TEX-MEX CHICKEN & RICE CHILI

Try this easy, one-dish chunky chili.

1 package (6.8 ounces) RICE-A-RONI Spanish Rice
2 cups chopped cooked chicken or turkey
1 can (15 or 16 ounces) kidney beans or pinto beans, rinsed and drained
1 can (14½ or 16 ounces) tomatoes or stewed tomatoes, undrained
1 medium green bell pepper, cut into ½-inch pieces
1½ teaspoons chili powder
1 teaspoon ground cumin
½ cup (2 ounces) shredded cheddar or monterey jack cheese (optional)
Sour cream (optional)
Chopped cilantro (optional)

1. In 3-quart saucepan, combine rice-vermicelli mix, contents of seasoning packet, 2¾ cups water, chicken, beans, tomatoes, green pepper, chili powder and cumin. Bring to a boil over high heat.

2. Reduce heat to low; simmer, uncovered, about 20 minutes or until rice is tender, stirring occasionally.

3. Top with cheese, sour cream and cilantro, if desired.   *4 servings*

Nutrition Information: ¼ RECIPE

Calories	410	Sodium	850 mg
Total Fat	7 g	Total Carbohydrates	54 g
Saturated Fat	1 g	Dietary Fiber	8 g
Cholesterol	60 mg	Protein	32 g

% Daily Value:

Vitamin A	25%	Calcium	10%
Vitamin C	60%	Iron	39%

BEEF SONOMA & RICE

Serve this easy beef dinner in any season.

1 pound lean ground beef (80% lean)
1 clove garlic, minced
1 package (6.8 ounces) RICE-A-RONI Beef Flavor
½ cup chopped green bell pepper *or* 1 can (4 ounces) chopped green chiles, undrained
¼ cup sliced green onions
1 medium tomato, chopped
2 tablespoons chopped parsley or cilantro

1. In large skillet, brown ground beef and garlic; drain. Remove from skillet; set aside.

2. In same skillet, prepare Rice-A-Roni Mix as package directs, stirring in beef mixture, green pepper and onions during last 5 minutes of cooking.

3. Sprinkle with tomato and parsley.   *4 servings*

Nutrition Information: ¼ RECIPE

Calories	450	Sodium	875 mg
Total Fat	22 g	Total Carbohydrates	38 g
Saturated Fat	7 g	Dietary Fiber	2 g
Cholesterol	70 mg	Protein	25 g

% Daily Value:

Vitamin A	16%	Calcium	3%
Vitamin C	34%	Iron	30%

Tex-Mex Chicken & Rice Chili

MEDITERRANEAN–STYLE CHICKEN & RICE

An easy dinner with lots of fresh flavor.

1 package (6.9 ounces) RICE-A-RONI Chicken Flavor
2 tablespoons margarine or butter
1 clove garlic, minced
2 tablespoons lemon juice
1 package (10 ounces) frozen chopped broccoli
2 cups chopped cooked chicken or turkey
½ teaspoon grated lemon peel

1. In round 3-quart microwaveable glass casserole, combine rice-vermicelli mix, margarine and garlic. Microwave on HIGH 3 to 3½ minutes or until vermicelli is golden brown, stirring after 2 minutes of cooking.

2. Stir in 2¾ cups water, lemon juice and contents of seasoning packet. Cover; microwave on HIGH 11 to 13 minutes.

3. Stir in frozen broccoli. Cover; microwave on HIGH 5 minutes.

4. Stir in chicken and lemon peel. Cover; microwave on HIGH 3 minutes or until most of liquid is absorbed and rice is tender.

5. Let stand 3 minutes. Stir before serving.   *4 servings*

Nutrition Information: ¼ RECIPE

Calories	370	Sodium	850 mg
Total Fat	12 g	Total Carbohydrates	40 g
Saturated Fat	2 g	Dietary Fiber	2 g
Cholesterol	65 mg	Protein	27 g
% Daily Value:			
Vitamin A	35%	Calcium	7%
Vitamin C	71%	Iron	25%

BEEF & BROCCOLI PEPPER STEAK

Always a favorite—beef with broccoli.

1 tablespoon margarine or butter
1 pound well-trimmed top round steak, cut into thin strips
1 package (6.8 ounces) RICE-A-RONI Beef Flavor
2 cups broccoli flowerets
½ cup red or green bell pepper strips
1 small onion, thinly sliced

1. In large skillet, melt margarine over medium meat. Add meat; sauté just until browned.

2. Remove from skillet; set aside. Keep warm.

3. In same skillet, prepare Rice-A-Roni Mix as package directs; simmer 10 minutes. Add meat and remaining ingredients; simmer an additional 10 minutes or until most of liquid is absorbed and vegetables are crisp-tender.

4 servings

Nutrition Information: ¼ RECIPE

Calories	420	Sodium	900 mg
Total Fat	13 g	Total Carbohydrates	41 g
Saturated Fat	3 g	Dietary Fiber	4 g
Cholesterol	65 mg	Protein	33 g
% Daily Value:			
Vitamin A	45%	Calcium	5%
Vitamin C	120%	Iron	37%

Beef & Broccoli Pepper Steak

TURKEY PARMESAN

*A perfect dinner the day after
Thanksgiving!*

²/₃ **cup milk**
**2 tablespoons margarine or
    butter**
2 cups zucchini slices, halved
**1 package (5.1 ounces)
    NOODLE RONI Angel Hair
    Pasta with Parmesan
    Cheese**
2 cups cooked turkey strips
**1 jar (2 ounces) chopped
    pimento, drained**
**2 tablespoons grated parmesan
    cheese**

1. In round 3-quart microwaveable
glass casserole, combine 1½ cups
water, milk, margarine and
zucchini. Microwave, uncovered,
on HIGH 6 minutes.

2. Stir in pasta, contents of
seasoning packet and turkey.
Separate pasta with a fork, if
needed.

3. Microwave, uncovered, on
HIGH 7 to 8 minutes, stirring after
2 minutes. Separate pasta with a
fork, if needed.

4. Sauce will be very thin, but will
thicken upon standing. Stir in
pimento and cheese.

5. Let stand 3 to 4 minutes or until
desired consistency. Stir before
serving.   *4 servings*

Nutrition Information: ¼ RECIPE

Calories	360	Sodium	675 mg
Total Fat	14 g	Total Carbohydrates	28 g
Saturated Fat	4 g	Dietary Fiber	2 g
Cholesterol	60 mg	Protein	29 g

% Daily Value:

Vitamin A	18%	Calcium	14%
Vitamin C	31%	Iron	22%

CHICKEN A LA PARMESANO

*Serve a spinach salad with this
saucy pasta dish.*

½ **cup milk**
**2 tablespoons margarine or
    butter**
**1 package (4.8 ounces)
    NOODLE RONI Parmesano**
**2 cups chopped cooked chicken
    or turkey**
**1 package (10 ounces) frozen
    corn *or* 1 can (16 or
    17 ounces) whole kernel
    corn, drained**
¼ **cup sliced green onions**
**1 jar (2 ounces) chopped
    pimento, drained**
1½ **teaspoons dried basil**

1. In round 3-quart microwaveable
glass casserole, combine 1²/₃ cups
water, milk and margarine.
Microwave, uncovered, on HIGH
4 to 5 minutes or until boiling.

2. Stir in pasta, contents of
seasoning packet, chicken, frozen
corn, onions, pimento and basil.

3. Microwave, uncovered, on
HIGH 11 to 12 minutes, stirring
gently after 5½ minutes.

4. Cover; let stand 3 to 4 minutes.
Sauce will thicken upon standing.
Stir before serving.   *4 servings*

Nutrition Information: ¼ RECIPE

Calories	400	Sodium	525 mg
Total Fat	15 g	Total Carbohydrates	40 g
Saturated Fat	3 g	Dietary Fiber	3 g
Cholesterol	70 mg	Protein	29 g

% Daily Value:

Vitamin A	17%	Calcium	10%
Vitamin C	31%	Iron	23%

Turkey Parmesan

PAELLA A LA ESPAÑOLA

*This traditional Spanish dish is
great for entertaining.*

**2 tablespoons margarine or
   butter**
**1¼ to 1½ pounds chicken thighs,
   skinned**
**1 package (7.2 ounces) RICE-A-
   RONI Rice Pilaf**
**1 can (14½ or 16 ounces)
   tomatoes or stewed
   tomatoes, undrained**
½ teaspoon turmeric (optional)
**⅛ teaspoon hot pepper sauce *or*
   black pepper**
**8 ounces medium cooked,
   shelled, deveined shrimp**
**1 cup frozen peas
   Lemon wedges**

1. In large skillet, melt margarine
over medium heat. Add chicken;
cook 2 minutes on each side or
until browned. Remove from
skillet; set aside, reserving
drippings. Keep warm.

2. In same skillet, sauté rice-pasta
mix in reserved drippings over
medium heat, until pasta is lightly
browned. Stir in 1½ cups water,
tomatoes, turmeric, hot pepper
sauce and contents of seasoning
packet. Bring to a boil over high
heat; stir in chicken.

3. Cover; reduce heat. Simmer 20
minutes. Stir in shrimp and frozen
peas.

4. Cover; continue to simmer 5 to
10 minutes or until liquid is
absorbed and rice is tender. Serve
with lemon wedges.   *4 servings*

Nutrition Information: ¼ RECIPE

Calories	470	Sodium	1250 mg
Total Fat	12 g	Total Carbohydrates	48 g
Saturated Fat	2 g	Dietary Fiber	3 g
Cholesterol	200 mg	Protein	42 g
% Daily Value:			
Vitamin A	24%	Calcium	10%
Vitamin C	43%	Iron	49%

Paella a la Española

TOMATO, BASIL & BROCCOLI CHICKEN

This colorful dinner is ready in just 30 minutes.

4 skinless, boneless chicken breast halves
  Salt and pepper (optional)
2 tablespoons margarine or butter
1 package (6.9 ounces) RICE-A-RONI Chicken Flavor
1 teaspoon dried basil
2 cups broccoli flowerets
1 medium tomato, seeded, chopped
1 cup (4 ounces) shredded mozzarella cheese

1. Sprinkle chicken with salt and pepper, if desired.

2. In large skillet, melt margarine over medium-high heat. Add chicken; cook 2 minutes on each side or until browned. Remove from skillet; set aside, reserving drippings. Keep warm.

3. In same skillet, sauté rice-vermicelli mix in reserved drippings over medium heat until vermicelli is golden brown. Stir in 2½ cups water, contents of seasoning packet and basil. Place chicken over rice mixture; bring to a boil over high heat.

4. Cover; reduce heat. Simmer 15 minutes. Top with broccoli and tomato.

5. Cover; continue to simmer 5 minutes or until liquid is absorbed and chicken is no longer pink inside. Sprinkle with cheese. Cover; let stand a few minutes before serving.   *4 servings*

Nutrition Information: ¼ RECIPE

Calories	460	Sodium	975 mg
Total Fat	14 g	Total Carbohydrates	41 g
Saturated Fat	5 g	Dietary Fiber	4 g
Cholesterol	90 mg	Protein	40 g
% Daily Value:			
Vitamin A	35%	Calcium	21%
Vitamin C	91%	Iron	27%

Tomato, Basil & Broccoli Chicken

30 MINUTE MAIN DISHES

CHICKEN RAGOÛT

A French bistro-style stew.

1 package (4.9 ounces) RICE-A-RONI Chicken & Broccoli Flavor
3 tablespoons all-purpose flour
¾ teaspoon salt (optional)
½ teaspoon black pepper
1 pound skinless, boneless chicken breasts or thighs, cut into 1-inch pieces
2 tablespoons margarine or butter
2 cups sliced mushrooms
1 cup thinly sliced carrots
1 cup coarsely chopped onion
2 cloves garlic, minced
½ cup reduced-sodium or regular chicken broth
¼ cup dry white wine or additional chicken broth
1 teaspoon dried thyme leaves

1. Prepare Rice-A-Roni Mix as package directs.

2. While Rice-A-Roni is simmering, combine flour, salt and pepper. Coat chicken with flour mixture.

3. In second large skillet, melt margarine over medium heat. Add mushrooms, carrots, onion and garlic; cook 5 minutes, stirring occasionally. Add chicken; continue cooking 4 minutes, stirring occasionally. Add chicken broth, wine and thyme. Reduce heat to low.

4. Simmer 5 to 7 minutes or until chicken is cooked through and carrots are tender.

5. Serve rice topped with chicken mixture. *4 servings*

Nutrition Information: ¼ RECIPE

Calories	400	Sodium	875 mg
Total Fat	11 g	Total Carbohydrates	38 g
Saturated Fat	2 g	Dietary Fiber	3 g
Cholesterol	65 mg	Protein	32 g

% Daily Value:

Vitamin A	165%	Calcium	6%
Vitamin C	15%	Iron	29%

Chicken Ragoût

ZESTY BARBECUED CHICKEN

The Southern barbecue seasoning tastes great!

1 package (6.5 ounces) RICE-A-RONI Broccoli Au Gratin
2 teaspoons paprika
1 teaspoon garlic powder
1/4 teaspoon celery salt (optional)
1/4 teaspoon freshly ground black pepper
1/8 teaspoon cayenne pepper (optional)
4 skinless, boneless chicken breast halves *or* well-trimmed center cut 1/2-inch-thick pork chops
1/4 cup barbecue sauce or hickory barbecue sauce

1. Prepare Rice-A-Roni Mix as package directs.

2. While Rice-A-Roni is simmering, combine seasonings; sprinkle evenly over both sides of chicken.

3. Place chicken on grill over medium coals *or* on rack of broiler pan. Grill or broil 3 to 4 inches from heat, 5 minutes. Brush with half of barbecue sauce. Turn; brush with remaining barbecue sauce.

4. Continue grilling or broiling 4 to 6 minutes or until chicken is no longer pink inside. Serve with rice.

4 servings

Nutrition Information: 1/4 RECIPE

Calories	390	Sodium	800 mg
Total Fat	13 g	Total Carbohydrates	34 g
Saturated Fat	3 g	Dietary Fiber	1 g
Cholesterol	70 mg	Protein	33 g

% Daily Value:

Vitamin A	25%	Calcium	7%
Vitamin C	8%	Iron	22%

MEXICALI BEEF & RICE

A new way to serve beef patties.

1 package (6.8 ounces) RICE-A-RONI Beef Flavor
1 cup frozen corn *or* 1 can (8 ounces) whole kernel corn, drained
1/2 cup chopped red or green bell pepper
1 pound lean ground beef (80% lean)
Salt and pepper (optional)
Salsa (optional)
Sour cream (optional)

1. Prepare Rice-A-Roni Mix as package directs, stirring in frozen corn and red pepper during last 10 minutes of cooking.

2. While Rice-A-Roni is simmering, shape beef into four 1/2-inch-thick patties.

3. In lightly greased second large skillet, cook beef patties over medium heat, about 4 minutes on each side or until desired doneness. Season with salt and pepper, if desired.

4. Serve rice topped with cooked beef patties, salsa and sour cream, if desired.

4 servings

Nutrition Information: 1/4 RECIPE

Calories	480	Sodium	875 mg
Total Fat	22 g	Total Carbohydrates	44 g
Saturated Fat	7 g	Dietary Fiber	2 g
Cholesterol	70 mg	Protein	26 g

% Daily Value:

Vitamin A	24%	Calcium	3%
Vitamin C	44%	Iron	29%

Mexicali Beef & Rice

SOUTHWEST CHICKEN

Cornmeal seals in the chicken's natural juices.

1 package (6.8 ounces) RICE-A-RONI Spanish Rice

½ cup chopped green bell pepper *or* 1 can (4 ounces) chopped green chiles, drained

1 can (14½ ounces) tomatoes, undrained, chopped

⅓ cup QUAKER or AUNT JEMIMA Yellow Corn Meal

1½ teaspoons chili powder

½ teaspoon garlic powder

4 skinless, boneless chicken breast halves

2 eggs, beaten

3 tablespoons vegetable oil

¼ cup (1 ounce) shredded cheddar or monterey jack cheese

1. Prepare Rice-A-Roni Mix as package directs, stirring in green pepper with water and tomatoes.

2. While Rice-A-Roni is simmering, combine corn meal, chili powder and garlic powder. Coat chicken with corn meal mixture; dip chicken into eggs, then coat again with corn meal mixture.

3. In second large skillet, heat oil over medium heat. Add chicken; cook 6 minutes on each side or until golden brown and no longer pink inside.

4. Serve rice topped with chicken; sprinkle with cheese. Cover; let stand a few minutes before serving.   *4 servings*

Nutrition Information: ¼ RECIPE

Calories	575	Sodium	875 mg
Total Fat	23 g	Total Carbohydrates	52 g
Saturated Fat	5 g	Dietary Fiber	4 g
Cholesterol	180 mg	Protein	39 g

% Daily Value:

Vitamin A	34%	Calcium	14%
Vitamin C	52%	Iron	33%

Southwest Chicken

QUICK STEAK DIANE

*A streamlined classic, elegant
enough for guests.*

**1 package (6.8 ounces) RICE-A-
    RONI Beef Flavor
4 (³/₄- to 1-inch-thick) top
    sirloin or tenderloin steaks
    (4 ounces *each*)
¹/₂ teaspoon freshly ground
    black pepper
1 tablespoon margarine or
    butter
1¹/₂ teaspoons Dijon mustard
1 tablespoon Worcestershire
    sauce
4 cups sliced mushrooms
¹/₂ cup finely chopped onion
¹/₄ cup reduced-sodium or
    regular beef broth
2 tablespoons chopped parsley**

1. Prepare Rice-A-Roni Mix as
package directs.

2. While Rice-A-Roni is simmering,
sprinkle meat with pepper. In
second large skillet, melt
margarine over medium-high heat;
cook steaks 2 minutes on each
side. Reduce heat to medium;
continue cooking 2 to 3 minutes
for medium-rare or until desired
doneness. Remove from skillet.
Spread with mustard; sprinkle
with Worcestershire sauce.

3. In same skillet, sauté
mushrooms and onion over
medium heat 2 to 3 minutes or
until tender.

4. Add beef broth; continue
cooking 2 minutes. Return meat
and meat juices to skillet. Cook
2 minutes or until heated through,
turning once.

5. Sprinkle with parsley; serve
with rice.   *4 servings*

Nutrition Information: ¹/₄ RECIPE

Calories	520	Sodium	1025 mg
Total Fat	27 g	Total Carbohydrates	41 g
Saturated Fat	8 g	Dietary Fiber	3 g
Cholesterol	75 mg	Protein	28 g

% Daily Value:

Vitamin A	13%	Calcium	4%
Vitamin C	10%	Iron	44%

CRISPY FISH FILLETS

*Cornmeal adds crunch to these
golden fish fillets.*

**1 package (7.2 ounces) RICE-A-
    RONI Herb & Butter
¹/₂ cup plain or seasoned dry
    bread crumbs
3 tablespoons QUAKER or
    AUNT JEMIMA Yellow
    Corn Meal
¹/₂ teaspoon salt (optional)
¹/₄ teaspoon black pepper
1 pound catfish, scrod or orange
    roughy fillets
2 tablepoons all-purpose flour
1 egg
2 tablespoons milk
2 tablespoons margarine or
    butter
2 tablespoons vegetable oil
4 lemon wedges**

1. Prepare Rice-A-Roni Mix as package directs.

2. While Rice-A-Roni is simmering, combine bread crumbs, corn meal, salt and pepper.

3. Cut fish into 4 serving size pieces. Coat fish with flour. Beat together egg and milk in separate dish; dip floured fish into egg mixture, then coat with corn meal mixture.

4. In second large skillet, heat margarine and oil over medium heat. Add fish; cook 4 to 5 minutes on each side or until golden brown and fish flakes easily with a fork; drain.

5. Serve rice topped with cooked fish. Serve with lemon wedges.

4 servings

Nutrition Information: ¼ RECIPE

Calories	500	Sodium	1350 mg
Total Fat	17 g	Total Carbohydrates	57 g
Saturated Fat	4 g	Dietary Fiber	2 g
Cholesterol	94 mg	Protein	26 g

% Daily Value:

Vitamin A	8%	Calcium	9%
Vitamin C	1%	Iron	23%

SWISS CHICKEN & RICE

Serve with a crunchy marinated vegetable salad.

1 package (4.9 ounces) RICE-A-RONI Chicken & Broccoli Flavor
1 tablespoon margarine or butter
4 skinless, boneless chicken breast halves, pounded to ½ inch thick
1 clove garlic, minced
1 tablespoon honey mustard or Dijon mustard
4 slices Swiss cheese

1. Prepare Rice-A-Roni Mix as package directs.

2. In second large skillet, melt margarine over medium heat. Add chicken and garlic. Cook 5 minutes. Turn; cook 2 minutes.

3. Spread mustard over chicken. Top with cheese. Continue cooking 3 to 4 minutes or until chicken is no longer pink inside and cheese is melted.

4. Serve rice topped with chicken.

4 servings

Nutrition Information: ¼ RECIPE

Calories	410	Sodium	825 mg
Total Fat	15 g	Total Carbohydrates	26 g
Saturated Fat	6 g	Dietary Fiber	1 g
Cholesterol	95 mg	Protein	39 g

% Daily Value:

Vitamin A	12%	Calcium	31%
Vitamin C	4%	Iron	17%

GLAZED PORK & RICE

Marmalade and vinegar make a sweet & sour glaze.

1 package (6.2 ounces) RICE-A-RONI Fried Rice
½ cup chopped onion
½ cup thinly sliced celery
2 cloves garlic, minced
¾ teaspoon ground ginger
1 pound pork tenderloin, sliced 1 inch thick
Salt (optional)
½ cup orange marmalade
1 tablespoon white wine vinegar or cider vinegar

1. In large skillet, prepare Rice-A-Roni Mix as package directs, sautéing onion, celery and garlic with rice-vermicelli mix and reducing water to 1¾ cups. Add ½ teaspoon ginger with water and contents of seasoning packet.

2. While Rice-A-Roni is simmering, cook pork in nonstick skillet, over medium heat 7 minutes on each side or until cooked through. Season with salt, if desired. Remove from skillet; set aside.

3. In same skillet, combine marmalade, vinegar and remaining ¼ teaspoon ginger. Cook over high heat 3 minutes or until thickened. Return cooked pork to skillet, turning to coat.

4. Serve rice topped with pork and sauce. *4 servings*

Nutrition Information: ¼ RECIPE

Calories	450	Sodium	1025 mg
Total Fat	10 g	Total Carbohydrates	63 g
Saturated Fat	2 g	Dietary Fiber	2 g
Cholesterol	70 mg	Protein	29 g
% Daily Value:			
Vitamin A	6%	Calcium	6%
Vitamin C	12%	Iron	29%

HERBED CHICKEN THIGHS

Savory seasonings make this simple dish special.

1½ teaspoons paprika
1 teaspoon dried thyme leaves
½ teaspoon garlic powder
½ teaspoon dried basil
½ teaspoon dried tarragon leaves *or* dried oregano leaves
8 small chicken thighs, skinned
2 tablespoons margarine or butter
1 package (5 ounces) RICE-A-RONI Chicken & Mushroom Flavor
2 cups sliced mushrooms
2 cloves garlic, minced

1. Combine seasonings. Sprinkle evenly on both sides of chicken.

2. In large skillet, melt margarine over medium heat. Add chicken; cook 25 to 30 minutes or until browned and no longer pink inside, turning occasionally.

3. While chicken is cooking, in second large skillet, prepare Rice-A-Roni Mix as package directs, sautéing mushrooms and garlic with rice-vermicelli mix.

4. Serve rice with chicken.

4 servings

Nutrition Information: ¼ RECIPE

Calories	330	Sodium	825 mg
Total Fat	12 g	Total Carbohydrates	29 g
Saturated Fat	2 g	Dietary Fiber	1 g
Cholesterol	95 mg	Protein	27 g
% Daily Value:			
Vitamin A	18%	Calcium	4%
Vitamin C	10%	Iron	28%

Glazed Pork & Rice

CHEESY CHICKEN & RICE FLORENTINE

This dish is certain to become a family favorite.

1 package (6.9 ounces) RICE-A-RONI Chicken Flavor
¼ cup dry bread crumbs
¼ cup grated parmesan cheese
1 egg
¼ cup milk
4 skinless, boneless chicken breast halves
¼ cup olive oil or vegetable oil
1 package (10 ounces) frozen chopped spinach, thawed, well drained

1. Prepare Rice-A-Roni Mix as package directs.

2. While Rice-A-Roni is simmering, combine bread crumbs and cheese. Beat together egg and milk in separate dish. Coat chicken in crumb mixture; dip into egg mixture, then coat again with crumb mixture.

3. In second large skillet, heat oil over medium heat. Add chicken; cook 6 minutes on each side or until golden brown and no longer pink inside.

4. Stir spinach into rice; heat through. Serve rice topped with chicken. *4 servings*

Nutrition Information: ¼ RECIPE

Calories	560	Sodium	1075 mg
Total Fat	25 g	Total Carbohydrates	44 g
Saturated Fat	5 g	Dietary Fiber	3 g
Cholesterol	130 mg	Protein	39 g

% Daily Value:

Vitamin A	118%	Calcium	22%
Vitamin C	32%	Iron	38%

PEPPERED STEAK WITH SAVORY RICE

A welcome alternative to meat and potatoes.

1 package (5.2 ounces) RICE-A-RONI Beef & Mushroom Flavor
1 pound well-trimmed 1-inch-thick top sirloin or top loin steak
1½ teaspoons cracked black pepper
2 cloves garlic, minced *or* ½ teaspoon garlic salt
1 large tomato, chopped

1. Prepare Rice-A-Roni Mix as package directs.

2. While Rice-A-Roni is simmering, evenly sprinkle both sides of meat with pepper and garlic; press seasonings into meat.

3. Grill over medium coals or broil 4 to 5 inches from heat, 5 to 6 minutes on each side for medium-rare or until desired doneness.

4. Thinly slice meat.

5. Stir tomato into rice; serve with meat. *4 servings*

Nutrition Information: ¼ RECIPE

Calories	420	Sodium	800 mg
Total Fat	21 g	Total Carbohydrates	30 g
Saturated Fat	7 g	Dietary Fiber	2 g
Cholesterol	75 mg	Protein	27 g

% Daily Value:

Vitamin A	8%	Calcium	3%
Vitamin C	13%	Iron	46%

Cheesy Chicken & Rice Florentine

CHICKEN CACCIATORE

A streamlined classic Italian chicken dish.

1 package (4.9 ounces) RICE-A-RONI Chicken & Broccoli Flavor
3 tablespoons all-purpose flour
1 teaspoon dried oregano leaves
½ teaspoon salt (optional)
¼ teaspoon black pepper
4 skinless, boneless chicken breast halves
1½ tablespoons olive oil or vegetable oil
1 medium onion, chopped
2 cloves garlic, minced
1 can (16 ounces) stewed tomatoes, undrained
1 large green bell pepper, chopped

1. Prepare Rice-A-Roni Mix as package directs.

2. While Rice-A-Roni is simmering, combine flour and seasonings in plastic bag. Add chicken pieces, one at a time, shaking to coat.

3. In second large skillet, heat oil over medium heat. Add chicken; cook 3 to 4 minutes or until golden brown. Turn; add onion and garlic. Continue cooking 3 to 4 minutes or until onion is crisp-tender.

4. Add tomatoes and green pepper. Cook, uncovered, about 8 minutes or until chicken is no longer pink inside and sauce is thickened, turning chicken after 4 minutes.

5. Serve rice topped with chicken mixture. *4 servings*

Nutrition Information: ¼ RECIPE

Calories	390	Sodium	1000 mg
Total Fat	10 g	Total Carbohydrates	41 g
Saturated Fat	1 g	Dietary Fiber	5 g
Cholesterol	70 mg	Protein	33 g

% Daily Value:

Vitamin A	21%	Calcium	9%
Vitamin C	69%	Iron	29%

BEEF, PEPPERS AND TOMATO STIR-FRY

This colorful meal is perfect for entertaining.

1 package (6.8 ounces) RICE-A-RONI Beef Flavor
1 pound well-trimmed top sirloin steak
¼ cup margarine or butter
Salt and pepper (optional)
½ red or green bell pepper, cut into strips
½ yellow bell pepper, cut into strips
1 medium onion, sliced
4 plum tomatoes, sliced into quarters
2 tablespoons dry red wine *or* 1 tablespoon Worcestershire sauce

1. Prepare Rice-A-Roni Mix as package directs.

2. While Rice-A-Roni is simmering, thinly slice meat across the grain.

3. In second large skillet, melt 2 tablespoons margarine over medium-high heat. Sauté meat 5 minutes or until no longer pink. Remove from skillet; sprinkle with salt and pepper, if desired. Set aside; keep warm.

4. In same skillet, sauté peppers and onion in remaining 2 tablespoons margarine 3 minutes or until crisp-tender. Stir in meat.

5. Meanwhile, add tomatoes and wine to rice during last 5 minutes of cooking. Serve rice topped with meat mixture.   *4 servings*

Nutrition Information: ¼ RECIPE

Calories	440	Sodium	950 mg
Total Fat	17 g	Total Carbohydrates	41 g
Saturated Fat	4 g	Dietary Fiber	3 g
Cholesterol	70 mg	Protein	30 g
% Daily Value:			
Vitamin A	30%	Calcium	4%
Vitamin C	59%	Iron	41%

TERIYAKI FISH KABOBS

Oriental sesame oil adds a lovely subtle flavor.

1 pound firm halibut, tuna or swordfish steaks *or* skinless, boneless chicken breast halves

1 large red or green bell pepper

4 green onions

1 package (4.9 ounces) RICE-A-RONI Chicken & Broccoli Flavor

1½ tablespoons reduced-sodium or regular soy sauce

2 tablespoons dry sherry or water

1 tablespoon Oriental sesame oil or vegetable oil

1 clove garlic, minced

1. Cut fish, red pepper and onions into 1-inch pieces.

2. Alternately thread fish, red pepper and onions onto 4 large skewers; set aside.

3. Prepare Rice-A-Roni Mix as package directs.

4. While Rice-A-Roni is simmering, combine soy sauce, sherry, oil and garlic. Brush kabobs with soy sauce mixture.

5. Grill over medium coals 14 minutes or broil 5 to 6 inches from heat 10 minutes, or until seafood is opaque, turning once and brushing with remaining soy sauce mixture.

6. Serve rice topped with kabobs.
                4 servings

Nutrition Information: ¼ RECIPE

Calories	330	Sodium	925 mg
Total Fat	9 g	Total Carbohydrates	29 g
Saturated Fat	1 g	Dietary Fiber	2 g
Cholesterol	35 mg	Protein	28 g
% Daily Value:			
Vitamin A	38%	Calcium	9%
Vitamin C	86%	Iron	22%

TURKEY CUTLETS WITH FRESH SALSA

Turkey breast slices are available in the meat case.

1 package (4.9 ounces) RICE-A-RONI Chicken & Broccoli Flavor
2 tablespoons all-purpose flour
½ teaspoon ground cumin
¼ teaspoon salt (optional)
⅛ teaspoon cayenne pepper or black pepper
1 pound fresh turkey breast slices, ¼ to ½ inch thick *or* 1 pound skinless, boneless chicken breast halves, pounded to ¼-inch thickness
2 tablespoons vegetable oil
2 cups chopped tomatoes
⅓ cup sliced green onions
2 tablespoons cider vinegar or white wine vinegar
2 tablespoons chopped cilantro or parsley

1. Prepare Rice-A-Roni Mix as package directs.

2. While Rice-A-Roni is simmering, combine flour and seasonings in a plastic bag. Add turkey slices, one at a time, shaking to coat.

3. In second large skillet, heat 1 tablespoon oil over medium heat. Add one-half of turkey slices. Cook 2 minutes on each side or until golden brown and no longer pink inside. Remove turkey from skillet onto serving platter; keep warm. Cook remaining turkey in remaining 1 tablespoon oil.

4. Stir tomatoes, onions and vinegar into skillet drippings. Cook 1 to 2 minutes or until thickened.

5. Pour tomato salsa mixture over turkey; sprinkle with cilantro. Serve with rice.　　　*4 servings*

Nutrition Information: ¼ RECIPE

Calories	370	Sodium	700 mg
Total Fat	11 g	Total Carbohydrates	33 g
Saturated Fat	2 g	Dietary Fiber	3 g
Cholesterol	70 mg	Protein	33 g

% Daily Value:

Vitamin A	17%	Calcium	5%
Vitamin C	33%	Iron	28%

Turkey Cutlets with Fresh Salsa

CHEESY DIJON CHICKEN

This tasty chicken dish is ready in 30 minutes.

1 package (6.2 ounces) RICE-A-RONI With 1/3 Less Salt Broccoli Au Gratin
2/3 cup dry bread crumbs
1 1/2 teaspoons dried basil
4 skinless, boneless chicken breast halves
4 teaspoons Dijon or prepared mustard
2 eggs, beaten
3 tablespoons vegetable oil
1/2 cup (2 ounces) shredded cheddar cheese

1. Prepare Rice-A-Roni Mix as package directs.

2. While Rice-A-Roni is simmering, combine bread crumbs and basil. Spread one side of each chicken breast with mustard. Coat chicken with bread crumb mixture; dip into beaten eggs, then coat again with bread crumb mixture.

3. In second large skillet, heat oil over medium heat. Add chicken; cook 6 minutes on each side or until golden brown and no longer pink inside.

4. Serve rice topped with chicken; sprinkle with cheese. Cover; let stand 5 minutes. *4 servings*

Nutrition Information: 1/4 RECIPE

Calories	580	Sodium	800 mg
Total Fat	27 g	Total Carbohydrates	43 g
Saturated Fat	7 g	Dietary Fiber	2 g
Cholesterol	190 mg	Protein	40 g

% Daily Value:

Vitamin A	13%	Calcium	21%
Vitamin C	5%	Iron	31%

GLAZED SHRIMP SKEWERS

Just three ingredients create this fabulous glaze.

1 package (6.5 ounces) RICE-A-RONI Broccoli Au Gratin
3 tablespoons apricot preserves
1 tablespoon lemon juice
1 teaspoon grated lemon peel
1 pound medium raw shrimp, shelled, deveined *or* large scallops, halved

1. Prepare Rice-A-Roni Mix as package directs.

2. Combine preserves, juice and 1/2 teaspoon lemon peel; set aside.

3. On 4 large skewers, thread shrimp. Brush both sides with preserve mixture.

4. Grill over medium coals *or* broil 5 to 6 inches from heat, 6 to 7 minutes for shrimp *or* 7 to 9 minutes for scallops, or until seafood is opaque, turning once.

5. Stir remaining 1/2 teaspoon lemon peel into rice. Serve with cooked seafood. *4 servings*

Nutrition Information: 1/4 RECIPE

Calories	370	Sodium	750 mg
Total Fat	12 g	Total Carbohydrates	42 g
Saturated Fat	3 g	Dietary Fiber	2 g
Cholesterol	140 mg	Protein	24 g

% Daily Value:

Vitamin A	8%	Calcium	10%
Vitamin C	7%	Iron	30%

Glazed Shrimp Skewer

SKILLET CHICKEN VESUVIO

A speedy version for classic Italian chicken.

1 package (6.9 ounces) RICE-A-RONI Chicken Flavor
12 unpeeled garlic cloves
3 tablespoons olive oil or vegetable oil
1½ teaspoons dried oregano leaves
½ teaspoon salt (optional)
½ teaspoon freshly ground black pepper
¼ teaspoon dried rosemary leaves (optional)
4 skinless, boneless chicken breast halves
1 medium tomato, chopped
4 lemon wedges (optional)

1. Prepare Rice-A-Roni Mix as package directs.

2. While Rice-A-Roni is simmering, combine garlic cloves and oil in second large skillet. Cover; cook over medium heat 5 minutes.

3. Combine seasonings; sprinkle over chicken.

4. Push garlic to edge of skillet. Add chicken; cook about 5 minutes on each side or until chicken is no longer pink inside. Remove garlic with slotted spoon. Squeeze softened garlic over chicken; discard garlic peels.

5. Stir tomato into rice. Serve rice topped with chicken, juices and lemon wedges. *4 servings*

Nutrition Information: ¼ RECIPE

Calories	460	Sodium	850 mg
Total Fat	18 g	Total Carbohydrates	40 g
Saturated Fat	3 g	Dietary Fiber	2 g
Cholesterol	70 mg	Protein	33 g

% Daily Value:

Vitamin A	10%	Calcium	6%
Vitamin C	17%	Iron	25%

Skillet Chicken Vesuvio

SHANGHAI FISH FILLETS

Serve this quick dish for a taste of the Orient.

1 package (6.1 ounces) RICE-A-RONI With 1/3 Less Salt Fried Rice
1/3 cup orange juice
1 1/2 tablespoons reduced-sodium or regular soy sauce
1 tablespoon firmly packed brown sugar
1/2 teaspoon ground ginger
1 pound orange roughy or scrod fillets
3 tablespoons all-purpose flour
2 tablespoons vegetable oil
1 clove garlic, minced
2 tablespoons sliced green onions (optional)

1. Prepare Rice-A-Roni Mix as package directs.

2. While Rice-A-Roni is simmering, combine orange juice, soy sauce, brown sugar and ginger; set aside.

3. Cut fish into four serving size pieces. Coat fish with flour.

4. In second large skillet, heat oil over medium heat. Add fish; cook 3 to 4 minutes on each side or until fish is golden brown and fish flakes easily with a fork. Remove fish to serving platter.

5. Add garlic to skillet; sauté 1 minute. Add orange juice mixture. Cook, stirring frequently, 3 to 4 minutes or until thickened. Pour over fish; sprinkle with onions. Serve with rice.   *4 servings*

Nutrition Information: 1/4 RECIPE

Calories	400	Sodium	875 mg
Total Fat	17 g	Total Carbohydrates	43 g
Saturated Fat	1 g	Dietary Fiber	1 g
Cholesterol	20 mg	Protein	22 g

% Daily Value:

Vitamin A	2%	Calcium	3%
Vitamin C	15%	Iron	15%

ONION SMOTHERED PORK CHOPS

When in season, use a sweet onion like Vidalia.

1 package (6.5 ounces) RICE-A-RONI Broccoli Au Gratin
4 well-trimmed 1/2- to 3/4-inch-thick center-cut loin pork chops
2 tablespoons coarse grain mustard or Dijon mustard
1 tablespoon margarine or butter
1 medium onion, thinly sliced, separated into rings
Salt (optional)
1/4 teaspoon freshly ground black pepper

1. Prepare Rice-A-Roni Mix as package directs.

2. While Rice-A-Roni is simmering, evenly spread both sides of pork chops with mustard.

3. In second large skillet, melt margarine over medium heat. Cook pork chops 6 minutes; turn. Top with onion rings. Cover; continue cooking 8 to 10 minutes or until pork is no longer pink inside. Remove pork from skillet onto serving platter.

4. Continue cooking onions over medium-high heat, 4 to 5 minutes or until softened and glazed, stirring constantly. Season with salt, if desired.

5. Spoon onions over pork and rice. Sprinkle with pepper before serving.   *4 servings*

Nutrition Information: 1/4 RECIPE

Calories	440	Sodium	925 mg
Total Fat	20 g	Total Carbohydrates	34 g
Saturated Fat	5 g	Dietary Fiber	2 g
Cholesterol	70 mg	Protein	30 g

% Daily Value:

Vitamin A	10%	Calcium	8%
Vitamin C	6%	Iron	19%

BROILED SHRIMP DE JONG

A flavorful lemon-garlic seafood dish.

1 package (4.9 ounces) RICE-A-RONI Chicken & Broccoli Flavor

1 pound large raw shrimp, shelled, deveined *or* large scallops

2 tablespoons lemon juice

3 tablespoons margarine or butter, melted

1 clove garlic, minced

1 teaspoon grated lemon peel

1/4 cup dry bread crumbs

2 tablespoons chopped parsley

1. Prepare Rice-A-Roni Mix as package directs.

2. While Rice-A-Roni is simmering, combine shrimp, lemon juice, 1 tablespoon melted margarine, garlic and 1/2 teaspoon lemon peel in 8- or 9-inch square baking pan.

3. Broil 5 to 6 inches from heat, 6 to 8 minutes for shrimp *or* 8 to 10 minutes for scallops, turning seafood after 3 minutes; stir.

4. Combine bread crumbs, parsley, remaining 2 tablespoons melted margarine and remaining 1/2 teaspoon lemon peel. Sprinkle over shrimp. Continue to broil about 1 minute or until crumbs are golden brown and seafood is opaque. Serve with rice.

4 servings

Nutrition Information: 1/4 RECIPE

Calories	350	Sodium	950 mg
Total Fat	14 g	Total Carbohydrates	32 g
Saturated Fat	2 g	Dietary Fiber	1 g
Cholesterol	140 mg	Protein	23 g

% Daily Value:

Vitamin A	13%	Calcium	9%
Vitamin C	9%	Iron	33%

EATING LIGHT

ROASTED VEGETABLES PROVENÇAL

Delicate flavors from the French region Provence.

8 ounces medium or large mushrooms, halved
1 large zucchini, cut into 1-inch pieces, halved
1 large yellow squash or additional zucchini, cut into 1-inch pieces, quartered
1 large red or green bell pepper, cut into 1-inch pieces
1 small red onion, cut into ¼-inch slices, separated into rings
3 tablespoons olive oil
2 cloves garlic, minced
1 teaspoon dried basil
1 teaspoon dried thyme leaves
½ teaspoon salt (optional)
¼ teaspoon freshly ground black pepper
4 large plum tomatoes, quartered
⅔ cup milk
2 tablespoons margarine or butter
1 package (5.1 ounces) NOODLE RONI Angel Hair Pasta with Parmesan Cheese

1. Heat oven to 425°F. In 15×10-inch jelly roll pan combine first 5 vegetables; add combined oil, garlic and seasonings. Toss to coat. Bake 15 minutes; stir in tomatoes. Continue baking 5 to 10 minutes or until vegetables are tender.

2. While vegetables are roasting, combine 1⅓ cups water, milk and margarine in medium saucepan; bring just to a boil. Gradually add pasta while stirring. Stir in contents of seasoning packet. Reduce heat to medium.

3. Boil, uncovered, stirring frequently, 4 minutes. Sauce will be very thin, but will thicken upon standing. Remove from heat.

4. Let stand 3 minutes or until desired consistency. Stir before serving. Serve noodles topped with vegetables.   *4 servings*

Nutrition Information: ¼ RECIPE

Calories	370	Sodium	600 mg
Total Fat	21 g	Total Carbohydrates	40 g
Saturated Fat	4 g	Dietary Fiber	4 g
Cholesterol	5 mg	Protein	10 g
% Daily Value:			
Vitamin A	49%	Calcium	13%
Vitamin C	122%	Iron	27%

Serving suggestion: Top each serving with ⅓ cup shredded cheddar cheese.

Roasted Vegetables Provençal

ORANGE GINGER CHICKEN & RICE

This is a mildly sweet & spicy Asian skillet dinner.

1 package (6.9 ounces) RICE-A-RONI With ⅓ Less Salt Chicken Flavor
1 tablespoon margarine or butter
1 cup orange juice
¾ pound skinless, boneless chicken breasts, cut into thin strips
2 cloves garlic, minced
¼ teaspoon ground ginger
Dash crushed red pepper flakes (optional)
1½ cups carrots, cut into short thin strips *or* 3 cups broccoli flowerets

1. In large skillet, sauté rice-vermicelli mix and margarine over medium heat, stirring frequently until vermicelli is golden brown.

2. Stir in 1½ cups water, orange juice, chicken, garlic, ginger, red pepper flakes and contents of seasoning packet; bring to a boil over high heat.

3. Cover; reduce heat. Simmer 10 minutes.

4. Stir in carrots.

5. Cover; continue to simmer 5 to 10 minutes or until liquid is absorbed and rice is tender.

4 servings

Nutrition Information: ¼ RECIPE

Calories	340	Sodium	575 mg
Total Fat	5 g	Total Carbohydrates	48 g
Saturated Fat	1 g	Dietary Fiber	3 g
Cholesterol	50 mg	Protein	25 g

% Daily Value:

Vitamin A	236%	Calcium	4%
Vitamin C	50%	Iron	20%

DEVILLED FISH FILLETS

Just four ingredients top this fish with flavor.

1 package (6.2 ounces) RICE-A-RONI With ⅓ Less Salt Broccoli Au Gratin
1 pound cod, scrod or orange roughy fillets
1 tablespoon lemon juice
1 tablespoon Dijon mustard
½ cup fresh bread crumbs *or* ¼ cup seasoned dry bread crumbs
Paprika (optional)
½ to ¾ teaspoon grated lemon peel
Lemon wedges

1. Prepare Rice-A-Roni Mix as package directs.

2. While Rice-A-Roni is simmering, heat oven to 425°F.

3. Place fish in single layer in 13×9-inch glass baking dish. Sprinkle with lemon juice; spread with mustard. Sprinkle with bread crumbs and paprika.

4. Bake 15 to 18 minutes or until fish flakes easily with a fork.

5. Stir lemon peel into rice; serve with fish and lemon wedges.

4 servings

Nutrition Information: ¼ RECIPE

Calories	330	Sodium	550 mg
Total Fat	11 g	Total Carbohydrates	32 g
Saturated Fat	2 g	Dietary Fiber	1 g
Cholesterol	50 mg	Protein	25 g

% Daily Value:

Vitamin A	9%	Calcium	5%
Vitamin C	6%	Iron	14%

Orange Ginger Chicken & Rice

GRILLED VEGETABLE KABOBS

Just as tasty whether grilled or broiled.

1 large red or green bell pepper
1 large zucchini
1 large yellow squash or additional zucchini
12 ounces large mushrooms
2 tablespoons olive oil
2 tablespoons red wine vinegar
1 package (7.2 ounces) RICE-A-RONI Herb & Butter
1 large tomato, chopped
¼ cup grated parmesan cheese

1. Cut red pepper into twelve 1-inch pieces. Cut zucchini and yellow squash crosswise into twelve ½-inch slices. Marinate red pepper, zucchini, yellow squash and mushrooms in combined oil and vinegar 15 minutes.

2. Alternately thread marinated vegetables onto 4 large skewers. Brush with any remaining oil mixture; set aside.

3. Prepare Rice-A-Roni Mix as package directs.

4. While Rice-A-Roni is simmering, grill kabobs over medium-low coals *or* broil 4 to 5 inches from heat 12 to 14 minutes or until tender and browned, turning once.

5. Stir tomato into rice. Serve rice topped with kabobs. Sprinkle with cheese.   *4 servings*

Nutrition Information: ¼ RECIPE

Calories	320	Sodium	1200 mg
Total Fat	10 g	Total Carbohydrates	50 g
Saturated Fat	2 g	Dietary Fiber	4 g
Cholesterol	5 mg	Protein	10 g

% Daily Value:

Vitamin A	42%	Calcium	14%
Vitamin C	114%	Iron	27%

Serving suggestion: Serve with ¾ cup nonfat or low-fat yogurt per serving.

QUICK FRIED RICE

Leftover pork roast or ham is the star here.

1 tablespoon vegetable oil
2 eggs, beaten
1 package (6.1 ounces) RICE-A-RONI With ⅓ Less Salt Fried Rice
½ teaspoon ground ginger
2 cups cooked pork or ham, cut into short thin strips
1 cup sliced mushrooms
3 green onions, cut into ½-inch slices

1. In large skillet, heat oil over medium heat. Add eggs. Cook without stirring, 2 minutes or until eggs are set. Loosen eggs from pan with spatula; slide onto plate. Cut egg mixture into short thin strips. Set aside; keep warm.

2. In same skillet, prepare Rice-A-Roni Mix as package directs, adding ginger with water and contents of seasoning packet. Bring to a boil over high heat. Cover; reduce heat. Simmer 15 minutes. Stir egg mixture, pork, mushrooms and onions into rice during last 5 minutes of cooking.

4 servings

Nutrition Information: ¼ RECIPE

Calories	390	Sodium	650 mg
Total Fat	15 g	Total Carbohydrates	34 g
Saturated Fat	4 g	Dietary Fiber	2 g
Cholesterol	160 mg	Protein	28 g

% Daily Value:

Vitamin A	5%	Calcium	5%
Vitamin C	6%	Iron	22%

Grilled Vegetable Kabobs

ANGEL HAIR AL FRESCO

White wine gives great flavor.

3/4 cup skim milk
1 tablespoon margarine or butter
1 package (4.8 ounces) NOODLE RONI Angel Hair Pasta with Herbs
1 can (6⅛ ounces) white tuna in water, drained, flaked *or* 1½ cups chopped cooked chicken
2 medium tomatoes, chopped
⅓ cup sliced green onions
¼ cup dry white wine or water
¼ cup slivered almonds, toasted (optional)
1 tablespoon chopped fresh basil *or* 1 teaspoon dried basil

1. In 3-quart saucepan, combine 1⅓ cups water, skim milk and margarine. Bring just to a boil.

2. Stir in pasta, contents of seasoning packet, tuna, tomatoes, onions, wine, almonds and basil. Return to a boil; reduce heat to medium.

3. Boil, uncovered, stirring frequently, 6 to 8 minutes. Sauce will be thin, but will thicken upon standing.

4. Let stand 3 minutes or until desired consistency. Stir before serving.   *4 servings*

Nutrition Information: ¼ RECIPE

Calories	250	Sodium	650 mg
Total Fat	6 g	Total Carbohydrates	30 g
Saturated Fat	1 g	Dietary Fiber	2 g
Cholesterol	20 mg	Protein	18 g

% Daily Value:

Vitamin A	13%	Calcium	9%
Vitamin C	24%	Iron	15%

HUEVOS CON ARROZ

Great for brunch or dinner.

1 package (6.8 ounces) RICE-A-RONI Spanish Rice
2 cups chopped tomatoes
4 eggs
½ cup (2 ounces) shredded cheddar cheese or monterey jack cheese
2 tablespoons chopped cilantro or parsley
¼ cup salsa or picante sauce (optional)

1. Prepare Rice-A-Roni Mix as package directs, substituting fresh tomatoes for 1 can (14½ ounces) tomatoes. Bring to a boil over high heat. Cover; reduce heat. Simmer 20 minutes.

2. Make 4 round indentations in rice with back of large spoon. Break 1 egg into each indentation. Cover; cook over low heat 5 to 7 minutes or until eggs are cooked to desired doneness.

3. Sprinkle with cheese and cilantro. Serve topped with salsa, if desired.   *4 servings*

Nutrition Information: ¼ RECIPE

Calories	370	Sodium	700 mg
Total Fat	16 g	Total Carbohydrates	41 g
Saturated Fat	5 g	Dietary Fiber	3 g
Cholesterol	230 mg	Protein	15 g

% Daily Value:

Vitamin A	30%	Calcium	16%
Vitamin C	35%	Iron	24%

Serving suggestion: *Serve with one 8-ounce glass of milk per serving.*

Angel Hair al Fresco

PASTA PRIMAVERA

An economical pasta dish.

1/2 cup milk
3 tablespoons margarine or
    butter
1 package (4.7 ounces)
    NOODLE RONI Fettuccine
2 cups broccoli flowerets
1 large red or green bell pepper,
    cut into 1/2-inch pieces
1 cup frozen peas
1 teaspoon dried basil
1 clove garlic, minced
1/4 cup grated parmesan cheese
    Freshly ground black pepper
    (optional)

1. In 3-quart saucepan, combine 1 1/4 cups water, milk and margarine.

2. Add pasta and contents of seasoning packet; bring just to a boil.

3. Add broccoli, red pepper, frozen peas, basil and garlic. Reduce heat to medium-low.

4. Boil, uncovered, stirring frequently, 8 to 9 minutes or until pasta is desired tenderness and broccoli is tender. Pasta will be saucy, but will thicken upon standing.

5. Sprinkle with cheese and pepper before serving.   *4 servings*

Nutrition Information: 1/4 RECIPE

Calories	300	Sodium	675 mg
Total Fat	15 g	Total Carbohydrates	33 g
Saturated Fat	4 g	Dietary Fiber	6 g
Cholesterol	10 mg	Protein	12 g
% Daily Value:			
Vitamin A	64%	Calcium	19%
Vitamin C	169%	Iron	20%

Serving suggestion: *Serve with a 1-ounce wedge of cheddar cheese or an 8-ounce glass of milk per serving.*

SANTA FE RICE SALAD

A zesty way to use leftover chicken or turkey.

1 package (6.9 ounces) RICE-A-
    RONI With 1/3 Less Salt
    Chicken Flavor
3 tablespoons vegetable oil
2 cups chopped cooked chicken
    or turkey
1 1/2 cups chopped tomato
1 cup frozen corn *or* 1 can
    (8 ounces) whole kernel
    corn, drained
1/2 cup chopped red or green bell
    pepper
1/4 cup sliced green onions
2 to 3 tablespoons chopped
    cilantro or parsley
2/3 cup salsa or picante sauce
2 tablespoons lime or lemon
    juice

1. Prepare Rice-A-Roni Mix as package directs, substituting 1 tablespoon oil for margarine. Cool 10 minutes.

2. In large bowl, combine prepared Rice-A-Roni, chicken, tomato, corn, red pepper, onions and cilantro.

3. Combine salsa, lime juice and remaining 2 tablespoons oil. Pour over rice mixture; toss. Cover; chill 4 hours or overnight. Stir before serving.   *5 servings*

Nutrition Information: 1/5 RECIPE

Calories	370	Sodium	625 mg
Total Fat	13 g	Total Carbohydrates	42 g
Saturated Fat	2 g	Dietary Fiber	3 g
Cholesterol	50 mg	Protein	22 g
% Daily Value:			
Vitamin A	25%	Calcium	3%
Vitamin C	93%	Iron	20%

Santa Fe Rice Salad

LOUISIANA RED BEANS & RICE

A traditional Cajun dish.

1 package (7.2 ounces) RICE-A-RONI Herb & Butter
1 cup chopped green or yellow bell pepper
¾ cup chopped onion
2 cloves garlic, minced
2 tablespoons vegetable oil or olive oil
1 can (15 or 16 ounces) red beans or kidney beans, rinsed and drained
1 can (14½ or 16 ounces) tomatoes or stewed tomatoes, undrained
1 teaspoon dried thyme leaves *or* dried oregano leaves
⅛ teaspoon hot pepper sauce *or* black pepper
2 tablespoons chopped parsley (optional)

1. Prepare Rice-A-Roni Mix as package directs.

2. While Rice-A-Roni is simmering, in second large skillet, sauté green pepper, onion and garlic in oil 5 minutes.

3. Stir in beans, tomatoes, thyme and hot pepper sauce. Simmer, uncovered, 10 minutes, stirring occasionally. Stir in parsley. Serve over rice.   *5 servings*

Nutrition Information: ⅕ RECIPE

Calories	330	Sodium	1175 mg
Total Fat	12 g	Total Carbohydrates	48 g
Saturated Fat	2 g	Dietary Fiber	6 g
Cholesterol	0 mg	Protein	9 g
% Daily Value:			
Vitamin A	17%	Calcium	9%
Vitamin C	56%	Iron	25%

Serving suggestion: Serve with one 8-ounce glass of milk per serving.

ORIENTAL MUSHROOM SOUP

The perfect soup for Cantonese food lovers.

1 tablespoon margarine or butter
4 cups sliced mushrooms
1 clove garlic, minced
3 cups water
1 can (13¾ ounces) reduced-sodium or regular chicken broth
½ cup sliced green onions
1 package (6.1 ounces) RICE-A-RONI With ⅓ Less Salt Fried Rice
1 tablespoon reduced-sodium or regular soy sauce
1 to 2 tablespoons lemon juice

1. In 3-quart saucepan, melt margarine over medium heat. Add mushrooms and garlic; sauté 3 to 4 minutes, stirring occasionally.

2. Add water, broth, onions, rice-vermicelli mix and contents of seasoning packet. Bring to a boil. Reduce heat.

3. Simmer 15 to 20 minutes or until rice is tender, stirring occasionally. Stir in soy sauce and lemon juice; heat through. Additional water may be added if soup thickens upon standing.   *4 servings*

Nutrition Information: ¼ RECIPE

Calories	220	Sodium	1025 mg
Total Fat	5 g	Total Carbohydrates	37 g
Saturated Fat	1 g	Dietary Fiber	2 g
Cholesterol	0 mg	Protein	6 g
% Daily Value:			
Vitamin A	4%	Calcium	3%
Vitamin C	12%	Iron	19%

Serving suggestion: Serve with one 8-ounce glass of milk per serving.

Louisiana Red Beans & Rice

STIR-FRY / EASY-BAKE DINNERS

SAVORY PORK & APPLE STIR-FRY

Apple juice gives the rice and sauce extra flavor.

1 package (7.2 ounces) RICE-A-RONI Rice Pilaf
1⅓ cups apple juice or apple cider
1 pound boneless pork loin, pork tenderloin *or* skinless, boneless chicken breast halves
1 teaspoon paprika
1 teaspoon dried thyme leaves
½ teaspoon ground sage *or* poultry seasoning
½ teaspoon salt (optional)
2 tablespoons margarine or butter
2 medium apples, cored, sliced
1 teaspoon cornstarch
⅓ cup coarsely chopped walnuts

1. Prepare Rice-A-Roni Mix as package directs, substituting 1 cup water and 1 cup apple juice for water in directions.

2. While Rice-A-Roni is simmering, cut pork into 1½ × ¼-inch strips. Combine seasonings; toss with meat.

3. In second large skillet, melt margarine over medium heat. Stir-fry meat 3 to 4 minutes or just until pork is no longer pink.

4. Add apples; stir-fry 2 to 3 minutes or until apples are almost tender. Add combined remaining ⅓ cup apple juice and cornstarch. Stir-fry 1 to 2 minutes or until thickened to form glaze.

5. Stir in nuts. Serve rice topped with pork mixture.   *4 servings*

Nutrition Information: ¼ RECIPE

Calories	600	Sodium	925 mg
Total Fat	25 g	Total Carbohydrates	62 g
Saturated Fat	5 g	Dietary Fiber	3 g
Cholesterol	65 mg	Protein	31 g

% Daily Value:

Vitamin A	18%	Calcium	8%
Vitamin C	66%	Iron	33%

Savory Pork & Apple Stir-Fry

SPEEDY STUFFED PEPPERS

This family favorite may be prepared ahead.

4 red, green or yellow bell peppers
3/4 pound lean ground beef (80% lean)
1/3 cup chopped onion
1 clove garlic, minced
1 package (6.8 ounces) RICE-A-RONI Beef Flavor
1/4 cup tomato paste
1/4 cup water
1 tablespoon brown sugar
3 tablespoons grated parmesan cheese (optional)

1. Cut peppers in half lengthwise; remove seeds and membranes. Cook in boiling water, 5 minutes; drain well. (Or, microwave in 13×9-inch glass baking dish, covered with plastic wrap, 5 minutes on HIGH.)

2. In large skillet, brown ground beef, onion and garlic; drain. Remove from skillet; set aside.

3. In same skillet, prepare Rice-A-Roni Mix as package directs.

4. Heat oven to 375°F. Place cooked peppers cut-side up in 13×9-inch glass baking dish. Combine rice and meat mixture; spoon into pepper halves. Combine tomato paste, water and brown sugar; spoon over rice mixture.

5. Tent with foil; bake 25 to 30 minutes or until heated through. Sprinkle with cheese, if desired.

4 servings

Nutrition Information: 1/4 RECIPE

Calories	440	Sodium	975 mg
Total Fat	18 g	Total Carbohydrates	47 g
Saturated Fat	6 g	Dietary Fiber	4 g
Cholesterol	50 mg	Protein	21 g
% Daily Value:			
Vitamin A	101%	Calcium	4%
Vitamin C	248%	Iron	31%

CANTON-STYLE FRIED RICE

Water chestnuts give a crunchy texture.

1 package (6.2 ounces) RICE-A-RONI Fried Rice
1 tablespoon vegetable oil
2 cups chopped cooked chicken, pork *or* shrimp
1 can (8 ounces) sliced water chestnuts *or* bamboo shoots, drained
1 egg, beaten
1/3 cup sliced green onions
Soy sauce (optional)

1. Prepare Rice-A-Roni Mix as package directs.

2. In wok or large skillet, heat oil over medium heat. Add prepared Rice-A-Roni, chicken and water chestnuts. Stir-fry until heated through.

3. Stir in egg and onions; continue stirring until egg is cooked. Serve with soy sauce, if desired.

4 servings

Nutrition Information: 1/4 RECIPE

Calories	420	Sodium	1025 mg
Total Fat	17 g	Total Carbohydrates	40 g
Saturated Fat	3 g	Dietary Fiber	1 g
Cholesterol	120 mg	Protein	27 g
% Daily Value:			
Vitamin A	8%	Calcium	5%
Vitamin C	5%	Iron	27%

Speedy Stuffed Peppers

PEANUT CHICKEN STIR-FRY

Peanut butter thickens and flavors the sauce.

1 package (6.1 ounces) RICE-A-RONI With ⅓ Less Salt Fried Rice
½ cup reduced-sodium or regular chicken broth
2 tablespoons creamy peanut butter
1 tablespoon reduced-sodium or regular soy sauce
1 tablespoon vegetable oil
¾ pound skinless, boneless chicken breasts, cut into ½-inch pieces
2 cloves garlic, minced
2 cups frozen mixed carrots, broccoli and red pepper vegetable medley, thawed, drained
2 tablespoons chopped peanuts (optional)

1. Prepare Rice-A-Roni Mix as package directs.

2. While Rice-A-Roni is simmering, combine chicken broth, peanut butter and soy sauce; mix with a fork. Set aside.

3. In second large skillet or wok, heat oil over medium-high heat. Stir-fry chicken and garlic 2 minutes.

4. Add vegetables and broth mixture; stir-fry 5 to 7 minutes or until sauce has thickened. Serve over rice. Sprinkle with peanuts, if desired.   *4 servings*

Nutrition Information: ¼ RECIPE

Calories	360	Sodium	925 mg
Total Fat	11 g	Total Carbohydrates	38 g
Saturated Fat	2 g	Dietary Fiber	2 g
Cholesterol	50 mg	Protein	27 g

% Daily Value:

Vitamin A	152%	Calcium	5%
Vitamin C	41%	Iron	20%

HARVEST STUFFED SQUASH

This is perfect for fall and winter.

2 medium acorn squash
1 package (6.5 ounces) RICE-A-RONI Broccoli Au Gratin
2 cups broccoli flowerets
1 cup (4 ounces) shredded cheddar cheese
½ cup chopped walnuts

1. Heat oven to 375°F. Cut squash in half lengthwise; remove seeds. Place cut-side down in 13×9-inch glass baking dish. Bake 30 minutes.

2. While squash is baking, prepare Rice-A-Roni Mix as package directs, stirring in broccoli during last 5 minutes of cooking. Stir ½ cup cheese and ¼ cup nuts into prepared rice mixture.

3. Turn squash cut-side up. Spoon rice mixture into squash halves. Sprinkle with remaining ½ cup cheese and ¼ cup nuts. Continue baking 15 to 20 minutes or until squash is tender.   *4 servings*

Nutrition Information: ¼ RECIPE

Calories	540	Sodium	800 mg
Total Fat	30 g	Total Carbohydrates	56 g
Saturated Fat	9 g	Dietary Fiber	10 g
Cholesterol	30 mg	Protein	18 g

% Daily Value:

Vitamin A	46%	Calcium	36%
Vitamin C	113%	Iron	30%

OVEN CHICKEN & RICE

There will only be one dish to wash after dinner!

1 package (4.3 ounces) RICE-A-RONI Long Grain & Wild Rice Pilaf
4 bone-in chicken breast halves
½ teaspoon dried thyme leaves *or* **dried basil**
¼ teaspoon garlic powder
1 tablespoon margarine or butter, melted
½ teaspoon paprika
1 cup chopped tomato *or* **red bell pepper**

1. Heat oven to 375°F. In 11×7-inch glass baking dish or 1½-quart casserole, combine 1¼ cups water, rice and contents of seasoning packet; mix well.

2. Place chicken over rice. Sprinkle evenly with thyme and garlic powder. Brush with margarine; sprinkle with paprika.

3. Cover with foil; bake 45 minutes. Stir in tomato. Bake, uncovered, 15 minutes or until liquid is absorbed and chicken is no longer pink inside. *4 servings*

Nutrition Information: ¼ RECIPE

Calories	280	Sodium	1000 mg
Total Fat	5 g	Total Carbohydrates	25 g
Saturated Fat	1 g	Dietary Fiber	1 g
Cholesterol	70 mg	Protein	31 g

% Daily Value:

Vitamin A	13%	Calcium	5%
Vitamin C	19%	Iron	16%

BEEF FRIED RICE

For a spicy dish add a dash of hot pepper sauce.

1 package (6.1 ounces) RICE-A-RONI With ⅓ Less Salt Fried Rice
¾ pound lean ground beef (80% lean)
½ cup thinly sliced celery
1 clove garlic, minced
3 tablespoons ketchup
1 tablespoon reduced-sodium or regular soy sauce
1 teaspoon Oriental sesame oil (optional)
2 tablespoons vegetable oil
1 large tomato, chopped
⅓ cup sliced green onions

1. Prepare Rice-A-Roni Mix as package directs.

2. While Rice-A-Roni is simmering, brown ground beef with celery and garlic in second large skillet; drain. Add ketchup, soy sauce and sesame oil; stir-fry 1 minute. Transfer to plate; set aside.

3. In same skillet, heat vegetable oil over medium heat. Add prepared Rice-A-Roni, tomato and onions; stir-fry 1 minute. Add meat mixture; stir-fry 2 minutes or until heated through. *4 servings*

Nutrition Information: ¼ RECIPE

Calories	480	Sodium	950 mg
Total Fat	27 g	Total Carbohydrates	38 g
Saturated Fat	8 g	Dietary Fiber	2 g
Cholesterol	65 mg	Protein	20 g

% Daily Value:

Vitamin A	7%	Calcium	5%
Vitamin C	18%	Iron	26%

LEMON-GARLIC SHRIMP

A savory stir-fry guaranteed to satisfy.

1 package (6.2 ounces) RICE-A-
   RONI With 1/3 Less Salt
   Broccoli Au Gratin
1 tablespoon margarine or
   butter
1 pound medium raw shrimp,
   shelled, deveined *or* large
   scallops, halved
1 medium red or green bell
   pepper, cut into short thin
   strips
2 cloves garlic, minced
1/2 teaspoon Italian seasoning
1/2 cup reduced-sodium or
   regular chicken broth
1 tablespoon lemon juice
1 tablespoon cornstarch
3 medium green onions, cut
   into 1/2-inch pieces
1 teaspoon grated lemon peel

1. Prepare Rice-A-Roni Mix as package directs.

2. While Rice-A-Roni is simmering, heat margarine in second large skillet or wok over medium-high heat. Add shrimp, red pepper, garlic and Italian seasoning. Stir-fry 3 to 4 minutes or until seafood is opaque.

3. Combine chicken broth, lemon juice and cornstarch, mixing until smooth. Add broth mixture and onions to skillet. Stir-fry 2 to 3 minutes or until sauce thickens.

4. Stir 1/2 teaspoon lemon peel into rice. Serve rice topped with shrimp mixture; sprinkle with remaining 1/2 teaspoon lemon peel.

4 servings

Nutrition Information: 1/4 RECIPE

Calories	340	Sodium	550 mg
Total Fat	12 g	Total Carbohydrates	34 g
Saturated Fat	2 g	Dietary Fiber	2 g
Cholesterol	140 mg	Protein	23 g

% Daily Value:

Vitamin A	30%	Calcium	9%
Vitamin C	68%	Iron	30%

Lemon-Garlic Shrimp

SOLE ALMONDINE

While dinner bakes, prepare a tossed salad.

1 package (6.5 ounces) RICE-A-RONI Broccoli Au Gratin
1 medium zucchini
4 sole, scrod or orange roughy fillets
1 tablespoon lemon juice
¼ cup grated parmesan cheese
Salt and pepper (optional)
¼ cup sliced almonds
2 tablespoons margarine or butter, melted

1. Prepare Rice-A-Roni Mix as package directs.

2. While Rice-A-Roni is simmering, cut zucchini lengthwise into 12 thin slices. Heat oven to 350°F.

3. In 11×7-inch glass baking dish, spread prepared rice evenly. Set aside. Sprinkle fish with lemon juice, 2 tablespoons cheese and salt and pepper, if desired. Place zucchini strips over fish; roll up. Place fish seam-side down on rice.

4. Combine almonds and margarine; sprinkle evenly over fish. Top with remaining 2 tablespoons cheese. Bake 20 to 25 minutes or until fish flakes easily with a fork. *4 servings*

Nutrition Information: ¼ RECIPE

Calories	460	Sodium	900 mg
Total Fat	22 g	Total Carbohydrates	34 g
Saturated Fat	5 g	Dietary Fiber	2 g
Cholesterol	60 mg	Protein	30 g

% Daily Value:

Vitamin A	17%	Calcium	17%
Vitamin C	10%	Iron	18%

GLAZED CORNISH HENS

These golden hens will make a dramatic dinner!

1 package (7.2 ounces) RICE-A-RONI Herb & Butter
1 package (9 ounces) frozen cut green beans
¼ teaspoon black pepper
2 cornish hens, split in halves *or* **1 broiler-fryer chicken (3 to 3½ pounds), quartered**
⅓ cup apricot or peach preserves
1 tablespoon Dijon mustard

1. Prepare Rice-A-Roni Mix as package directs. Add frozen green beans and pepper, stirring just until beans are separated.

2. Heat oven to 400°F. Spoon rice mixture into 11×7-inch glass baking dish; top with hen halves. Bake 30 minutes.

3. Combine preserves and mustard; brush hens with preserve mixture.

4. Continue baking 15 to 25 minutes or until hens are no longer pink inside and glaze is golden brown. *4 servings*

Nutrition Information: ¼ RECIPE

Calories	620	Sodium	1400 mg
Total Fat	24 g	Total Carbohydrates	61 g
Saturated Fat	6 g	Dietary Fiber	2 g
Cholesterol	110 mg	Protein	40 g

% Daily Value:

Vitamin A	16%	Calcium	10%
Vitamin C	19%	Iron	30%

Glazed Cornish Hen

ORIENTAL BEEF

East meets West in this quick stir-fry.

1 package (6.8 ounces) RICE-A-RONI Beef Flavor
1 pound, well-trimmed top sirloin steak, 3/4 to 1 inch thick
2 cloves garlic, minced
1/2 teaspoon ground ginger
1 tablespoon vegetable oil
3 cups broccoli flowerets
1/4 cup water
2 tablespoons reduced-sodium or regular soy sauce
2 teaspoons cornstarch
2 tablespoons dry sherry or water

1. Prepare Rice-A-Roni Mix as package directs.

2. While Rice-A-Roni is simmering, cut meat across the grain into 1/8-inch strips; cut each strip into 2-inch pieces. In small bowl, toss meat with garlic and ginger.

3. In second large skillet or wok, heat oil over medium heat. Stir-fry meat mixture 5 to 7 minutes or until meat is slightly pink in center. Remove from skillet; set aside.

4. Add broccoli and water to skillet; cover and steam 3 to 5 minutes or until crisp-tender.

5. While broccoli is steaming, combine soy sauce and cornstarch, mixing until smooth; stir in sherry.

6. Add meat and soy sauce mixture to broccoli. Stir-fry 2 minutes or until sauce has thickened. Serve rice topped with meat and broccoli.   *4 servings*

Nutrition Information: 1/4 RECIPE

Calories	450	Sodium	1200 mg
Total Fat	15 g	Total Carbohydrates	43 g
Saturated Fat	3 g	Dietary Fiber	5 g
Cholesterol	70 mg	Protein	33 g

% Daily Value:

Vitamin A	39%	Calcium	7%
Vitamin C	118%	Iron	46%

BANGKOK PORK

This Asian dish is just as tasty with chicken.

1 package (6.1 ounces) RICE-A-RONI With 1/3 Less Salt Fried Rice
1 tablespoon vegetable oil
1 pound lean boneless pork loin or tenderloin *or* skinless, boneless chicken breasts, cut into short thin strips
2 cloves garlic, minced
2 cups fresh pea pods, halved *or* 1 package (6 ounces) frozen pea pods
1 can (8 ounces) sliced water chestnuts *or* bamboo shoots, drained
1/2 cup reduced-sodium or regular chicken broth
1 tablespoon reduced-sodium or regular soy sauce
1 tablespoon cornstarch

1. Prepare Rice-A-Roni Mix as package directs.

2. While Rice-A-Roni is simmering, heat oil in wok or second large skillet over medium-high heat. Stir-fry pork and garlic 2 minutes.

3. Add pea pods and water chestnuts; stir-fry 3 to 4 minutes or until pork is no longer pink and pea pods are crisp-tender.

4. Combine broth, soy sauce and cornstarch, mixing until smooth. Add to pork mixture; stir-fry 2 to 3 minutes or until sauce has thickened. Serve over rice.

4 servings

Nutrition Information: ¼ RECIPE

Calories	430	Sodium	900 mg
Total Fat	12 g	Total Carbohydrates	47 g
Saturated Fat	3 g	Dietary Fiber	3 g
Cholesterol	75 mg	Protein	32 g

% Daily Value:

Vitamin A	4%	Calcium	8%
Vitamin C	77%	Iron	35%

SCALLOPED CHICKEN & PASTA

A mixed fruit salad will complement this dish.

¼ **cup margarine or butter**
1 **package (6.2 ounces) NOODLE RONI Shells & White Cheddar**
2 **cups frozen mixed vegetables**
⅔ **cup milk**
2 **cups chopped cooked chicken** *or* **ham**
¼ **cup dry bread crumbs**

1. Heat oven to 450°F.

2. In 3-quart saucepan, combine 2¼ cups water and 2 tablespoons margarine. Bring just to a boil. Stir in pasta and frozen vegetables. Reduce heat to medium.

3. Boil, uncovered, stirring frequently, 12 to 14 minutes or until most of water is absorbed. Add milk, contents of seasoning packet and chicken. Continue cooking 3 minutes.

4. Meanwhile, melt remaining 2 tablespoons margarine; stir in bread crumbs.

5. Transfer pasta mixture to 8- or 9-inch square glass baking dish. Sprinkle with bread crumbs. Bake 10 minutes or until bread crumbs are browned and edges are bubbly. *4 servings*

Nutrition Information: ¼ RECIPE

Calories	510	Sodium	850 mg
Total Fat	23 g	Total Carbohydrates	47 g
Saturated Fat	6 g	Dietary Fiber	4 g
Cholesterol	70 mg	Protein	31 g

% Daily Value:

Vitamin A	104%	Calcium	19%
Vitamin C	17%	Iron	30%

SWEET & SOUR CHICKEN

A healthier dish without the deep fat frying.

1 package (6.1 ounces) RICE-A-RONI With 1/3 Less Salt Fried Rice
2 tablespoons vegetable oil
1 pound skinless, boneless chicken breasts *or* pork tenderloin, cut into short, thin strips
2 cloves garlic, minced
2 medium carrots, sliced
1 large green bell pepper, cut into 1-inch pieces
1 can (8 ounces) pineapple chunks in juice, drained, reserving 1/4 cup juice
3 tablespoons prepared stir-fry sauce
1 tablespoon vinegar

1. Prepare Rice-A-Roni Mix as package directs.

2. While Rice-A-Roni is simmering, heat 1 tablespoon oil in wok or second large skillet over medium-high heat. Stir-fry chicken and garlic 3 minutes or until chicken is no longer pink; drain. Remove from wok; set aside.

3. Heat remaining 1 tablespoon oil in wok. Stir-fry carrots and green pepper 4 to 5 minutes or until crisp-tender.

4. Add cooked chicken, pineapple, reserved pineapple juice, stir-fry sauce and vinegar. Stir-fry 1 minute or until sauce has thickened. Serve over rice.

4 servings

Nutrition Information: 1/4 RECIPE

Calories	420	Sodium	950 mg
Total Fat	11 g	Total Carbohydrates	52 g
Saturated Fat	2 g	Dietary Fiber	3 g
Cholesterol	65 mg	Protein	32 g

% Daily Value:

Vitamin A	208%	Calcium	5%
Vitamin C	56%	Iron	20%

BAKED CHICKEN & RICE FRITTATA

This is an Italian crustless quiche.

1 package (5 ounces) RICE-A-RONI Chicken & Mushroom Flavor
3 eggs
2 cups chopped cooked chicken
1 cup milk
1/2 cup sliced green onions
1 teaspoon dried tarragon leaves *or* dried basil
1/4 teaspoon black pepper

1. Prepare Rice-A-Roni Mix as package directs. Heat oven to 375°F. Grease 9-inch square glass baking dish.

2. In large bowl, beat eggs. Add chicken, milk, onions, seasonings and prepared rice; mix well.

3. Pour into prepared baking dish. Bake 30 to 35 minutes or until knife inserted in center comes out clean. Let stand 5 minutes before serving. *4 servings*

Nutrition Information: 1/4 RECIPE

Calories	380	Sodium	850 mg
Total Fat	17 g	Total Carbohydrates	28 g
Saturated Fat	4 g	Dietary Fiber	1 g
Cholesterol	220 mg	Protein	29 g

% Daily Value:

Vitamin A	13%	Calcium	6%
Vitamin C	4%	Iron	24%

Sweet & Sour Chicken

SOUPS & SALADS

TUNA PILAF SALAD

This salad is delicious either warm or chilled.

1 package (7.2 ounces) RICE-A-RONI Rice Pilaf

1 package (10 ounces) frozen cut green beans

1 small red onion, thinly sliced, slices halved

¼ cup Italian dressing

2 cans (6⅛ ounces *each*) white tuna in water, drained, flaked

½ cup ripe pitted olives (optional)

1 large tomato, cut into 12 wedges

1 tablespoon chopped parsley

1. Prepare Rice-A-Roni Mix as package directs, reducing water to 1¾ cups and stirring in frozen green beans and onion during last 15 minutes of cooking.

2. Remove from heat; stir in dressing.

3. Top rice mixture with tuna, olives, tomato and parsley.

4. Serve warm or chilled with additional dressing, if desired.

5 servings

Nutrition Information: ⅕ RECIPE

Calories	360	Sodium	1000 mg
Total Fat	13 g	Total Carbohydrates	40 g
Saturated Fat	2 g	Dietary Fiber	2 g
Cholesterol	25 mg	Protein	23 g

% Daily Value:

Vitamin A	14%	Calcium	6%
Vitamin C	27%	Iron	21%

Tuna Pilaf Salad

CREAMY FETTUCCINE SOUP

Vegetable-noodle soup was never more delicious!

1 can (10½ ounces) condensed chicken broth
1¼ cups water
1 medium carrot, thinly sliced
1 package (4.7 ounces) NOODLE RONI Fettuccine
2 cups milk
1½ cups broccoli flowerets
½ teaspoon dried basil
2 tablespoons chopped parsley *or* chives
½ cup croutons (optional)

1. In 3-quart saucepan, combine chicken broth, water and carrot. Bring to a boil over high heat; simmer 3 minutes.

2. Stir in pasta, contents of seasoning packet, milk, broccoli and basil. Bring just to a boil; reduce heat.

3. Boil, uncovered, over medium-low heat, stirring frequently, 9 to 11 minutes or until pasta is desired tenderness.

4. Ladle into soup bowls; sprinkle with parsley. Top with croutons, if desired.   *4 servings*

Nutrition Information: ¼ RECIPE

Calories	250	Sodium	950 mg
Total Fat	8 g	Total Carbohydrates	32 g
Saturated Fat	4 g	Dietary Fiber	4 g
Cholesterol	20 mg	Protein	14 g
% Daily Value:			
Vitamin A	122%	Calcium	21%
Vitamin C	66%	Iron	17%

Serving suggestion: Serve with one 8-ounce glass of milk per serving.

ITALIAN PEASANT SALAD

Classic Tuscan flavor from the old country.

1 package (6.9 ounces) RICE-A-RONI Chicken Flavor
2 tablespoons vegetable oil
1 can (14 to 16 ounces) great northern beans, navy beans or cannellini beans, rinsed, drained
2 cups chopped cooked chicken
2 cups chopped tomato
1 cup frozen peas
½ cup Italian dressing
1 teaspoon dried basil *or* ½ teaspoon dried rosemary leaves

1. Prepare Rice-A-Roni Mix as package directs, substituting oil for margarine. Cool 10 minutes.

2. In large bowl, combine prepared Rice-A-Roni, beans, chicken, tomato, frozen peas, dressing and basil. Chill 4 hours or overnight. Stir before serving.   *6 servings*

VARIATION: Substitute 2 cans (6⅛ ounces *each*) white tuna in water, drained, flaked, for chicken.

Nutrition Information: ⅙ RECIPE

Calories	410	Sodium	775 mg
Total Fat	19 g	Total Carbohydrates	40 g
Saturated Fat	3 g	Dietary Fiber	5 g
Cholesterol	40 mg	Protein	22 g
% Daily Value:			
Vitamin A	12%	Calcium	5%
Vitamin C	28%	Iron	26%

Italian Peasant Salad

WHITE CHEDDAR SEAFOOD CHOWDER

Great with oyster crackers or crisp bread sticks.

2 tablespoons margarine or butter
½ cup chopped onion
2¼ cups water
1 package (6.2 ounces) NOODLE RONI Shells & White Cheddar
1 cup sliced carrots
½ teaspoon salt (optional)
¾ pound fresh *or* thawed frozen firm white fish, cut into ½-inch pieces
1¼ cups milk
2 tablespoons chopped parsley (optional)

1. In 3-quart saucepan, melt margarine over medium heat. Add onion; sauté 1 minute.

2. Add water; bring to a boil over high heat.

3. Stir in pasta, carrots and salt.

4. Bring just to a boil. Reduce heat to medium. Boil, uncovered, stirring frequently, 12 minutes.

5. Add fish, milk, parsley and contents of seasoning packet. Continue cooking 3 to 4 minutes, stirring occasionally, or until pasta is desired tenderness and fish is opaque.   *4 servings*

Nutrition Information: ¼ RECIPE

Calories	400	Sodium	675 mg
Total Fat	17 g	Total Carbohydrates	35 g
Saturated Fat	5 g	Dietary Fiber	1 g
Cholesterol	65 mg	Protein	25 g

% Daily Value:

Vitamin A	162%	Calcium	19%
Vitamin C	8%	Iron	16%

REFRESHING CHICKEN & RICE SALAD

Perfect for a picnic or pot luck supper.

1 package (4.3 ounces) RICE-A-RONI Long Grain & Wild Rice Pilaf
1 tablespoon vegetable oil
2 cups chopped cooked chicken
2 carrots, sliced lengthwise, cut into slices
1 cucumber, peeled, seeded, cut into short thin strips
½ cup red or green bell pepper, cut into short thin strips
2 tablespoons sliced green onions
⅓ cup Italian dressing
Lettuce

1. Prepare Rice-A-Roni Mix as package directs, substituting oil for margarine. Cool 10 minutes.

2. In large bowl, combine prepared Rice-A-Roni, chicken, carrots, cucumber, red pepper, onions and dressing. Chill 4 hours or overnight. Stir before serving.

3. Serve on lettuce-lined platter.

5 servings

Nutrition Information: ⅕ RECIPE

Calories	300	Sodium	850 mg
Total Fat	13 g	Total Carbohydrates	24 g
Saturated Fat	2 g	Dietary Fiber	2 g
Cholesterol	50 mg	Protein	20 g

% Daily Value:

Vitamin A	175%	Calcium	5%
Vitamin C	46%	Iron	13%

Refreshing Chicken & Rice Salad

CORN, BACON & RICE CHOWDER

Perfect comfort food on a chilly day.

- 1 package (7.2 ounces) RICE-A-RONI Rice Pilaf
- 2 tablespoons margarine or butter
- 1 can (13¾ ounces) reduced-sodium or regular chicken broth
- 1½ cups frozen corn *or* 1 can (16 or 17 ounces) whole kernel corn, drained
- 1 cup milk
- 1 cup water
- ½ cup sliced green onions
- 2 slices crisply cooked bacon, crumbled

1. In 3-quart saucepan, sauté rice-pasta mix and margarine over medium heat, stirring frequently until pasta is lightly browned.

2. Stir in chicken broth and contents of seasoning packet; bring to a boil over high heat.

3. Cover; reduce heat. Simmer 8 minutes.

4. Stir in frozen corn, milk, water and onions. Simmer, uncovered, 10 to 12 minutes, stirring occasionally. Stir in bacon before serving.

4 servings

Nutrition Information: ¼ RECIPE

Calories	360	Sodium	1150 mg
Total Fat	11 g	Total Carbohydrates	55 g
Saturated Fat	3 g	Dietary Fiber	2 g
Cholesterol	14 mg	Protein	10 g
% Daily Value:			
Vitamin A	9%	Calcium	11%
Vitamin C	13%	Iron	19%

Serving suggestion: Serve with a 1½-ounce wedge of cheddar cheese per serving.

TANGY LEMON CHICKEN SALAD

Lemon juice adds a piquant flavor to this salad.

- 1 package (4.3 ounces) RICE-A-RONI Long Grain & Wild Rice Pilaf
- 5 tablespoons vegetable oil or olive oil
- 2 cups chopped cooked chicken
- ¼ cup sliced green onions
- 3 tablespoons lemon juice
- ½ teaspoon grated lemon peel
- 1½ cups shredded spinach leaves *or* romaine lettuce leaves

1. Prepare Rice-A-Roni Mix as package directs, substituting 1 tablespoon oil for margarine. Cool 10 minutes.

2. In large bowl, combine prepared Rice-A-Roni, remaining 4 tablespoons oil, chicken, onions, lemon juice and lemon peel. Chill 4 hours or overnight.

3. Stir in spinach just before serving.

4 servings

Nutrition Information: ¼ RECIPE

Calories	400	Sodium	950 mg
Total Fat	23 g	Total Carbohydrates	24 g
Saturated Fat	4 g	Dietary Fiber	1 g
Cholesterol	60 mg	Protein	24 g
% Daily Value:			
Vitamin A	30%	Calcium	7%
Vitamin C	19%	Iron	18%

Corn, Bacon & Rice Chowder

HOPPIN' JOHN RICE SALAD

Inspired by the traditional Southern dish.

1 package (6.9 ounces) RICE-A-RONI Chicken Flavor
6 tablespoons vegetable oil
1 teaspoon dried thyme or marjoram
1 can (16 ounces) black-eyed peas, rinsed, drained
2 cups chopped cooked chicken *or* ham
1 cup red or green bell pepper strips
½ cup sliced green onions
3 tablespoons lemon juice
¼ teaspoon hot pepper sauce (optional)

1. Prepare Rice-A-Roni Mix as package directs, substituting 1 tablespoon oil for margarine and stirring in thyme with water and contents of seasoning packet. Cool 10 minutes.

2. In large bowl, combine prepared Rice-A-Roni, peas, chicken, red pepper, onions, lemon juice and hot pepper sauce with remaining 5 tablespoons oil. Chill 4 hours or overnight. Stir before serving.

4 servings

Nutrition Information: ¼ RECIPE

Calories	570	Sodium	900 mg
Total Fat	28 g	Total Carbohydrates	50 g
Saturated Fat	4 g	Dietary Fiber	5 g
Cholesterol	65 mg	Protein	30 g
% Daily Value:			
Vitamin A	31%	Calcium	7%
Vitamin C	89%	Iron	37%

GREEK RICE SALAD

Feta gives this salad its mildly robust flavor.

1 package (7.2 ounces) RICE-A-RONI Rice Pilaf
1 cup chopped cucumber
1 cup crumbled feta cheese or cubed brick or monterey jack cheese
¼ cup chopped parsley
⅓ cup olive oil or vegetable oil
3 tablespoons red wine vinegar *or* lemon juice
1 clove garlic, minced
2 teaspoons dried oregano leaves or dried mint
1 large tomato, chopped

1. Prepare Rice-A-Roni Mix as package directs. Cool 10 minutes.

2. In large bowl, combine prepared Rice-A-Roni, cucumber, cheese and parsley.

3. Combine oil, vinegar, garlic and oregano. Pour over rice mixture; toss. Cover; chill 4 hours or overnight. Stir in tomato just before serving.

5 servings

Nutrition Information: ⅕ RECIPE

Calories	400	Sodium	950 mg
Total Fat	25 g	Total Carbohydrates	35 g
Saturated Fat	7 g	Dietary Fiber	1 g
Cholesterol	25 mg	Protein	8 g
% Daily Value:			
Vitamin A	12%	Calcium	17%
Vitamin C	16%	Iron	18%

Serving suggestion: *Serve with 1 cup plain yogurt, topped with a little honey per serving.*

Greek Rice Salad

CHICKEN NOODLE & VEGETABLE SOUP

After this you may never open another can of soup!

2 tablespoons margarine or butter
3/4 pound skinless, boneless chicken breasts or thighs, cut into 1/2-inch pieces
1 cup chopped onion
2 cups frozen mixed broccoli, cauliflower and carrots vegetable medley
1 can (13 3/4 ounces) reduced-sodium or regular chicken broth
1/4 teaspoon dried thyme leaves *or* dried basil
1/8 teaspoon black pepper
1 package (4.7 ounces) NOODLE RONI Linguini Pasta with Chicken & Broccoli

1. In 3-quart saucepan, melt margarine over medium heat. Add chicken and onion; cook, stirring occasionally, 4 to 5 minutes or until chicken is no longer pink.

2. Add 1 1/2 cups water, frozen vegetables, chicken broth and seasonings. Bring just to a boil.

3. Gradually add pasta while stirring. Separate pasta with a fork, if needed.

4. Stir in contents of seasoning packet.

5. Boil, uncovered, stirring frequently, 9 to 10 minutes or until pasta is desired tenderness.

4 servings

Nutrition Information: 1/4 RECIPE

Calories	320	Sodium	800 mg
Total Fat	9 g	Total Carbohydrates	30 g
Saturated Fat	2 g	Dietary Fiber	4 g
Cholesterol	50 mg	Protein	27 g

% Daily Value:

Vitamin A	110%	Calcium	7%
Vitamin C	58%	Iron	19%

HAWAIIAN SHRIMP SALAD

Serve over lettuce leaves for even more color.

1 package (6.2 ounces) RICE-A-RONI Fried Rice
2 tablespoons vegetable oil
1 package (10 ounces) frozen cleaned precooked shrimp, thawed, drained
1 can (8 ounces) pineapple tidbits or chunks in juice, drained, reserving 1/3 cup juice
1 cup chopped red, yellow or green bell pepper
2/3 cup sliced green onions
1/2 cup plain nonfat yogurt or low-fat yogurt

1. Prepare Rice-A-Roni Mix as package directs, substituting oil for margarine. Cool 10 minutes.

2. In large bowl, combine prepared Rice-A-Roni, shrimp, pineapple, reserved pineapple juice, red pepper, onions and yogurt. Chill 4 hours or overnight. Stir before serving.

4 servings

Nutrition Information: 1/4 RECIPE

Calories	350	Sodium	1050 mg
Total Fat	9 g	Total Carbohydrates	46 g
Saturated Fat	1 g	Dietary Fiber	3 g
Cholesterol	140 mg	Protein	22 g

% Daily Value:

Vitamin A	31%	Calcium	13%
Vitamin C	95%	Iron	36%

INDEX

INDEX